How to Do Things with International Law

Ian Hurd

PRINCETON UNIVERSITY PRESS

PRINCETON AND OXFORD

Published by Princeton University Press,
41 William Street, Princeton, New Jersey 08540

In the United Kingdom: Princeton University Press,
6 Oxford Street, Woodstock, Oxfordshire OX20 1TR

press.princeton.edu

Library of Congress Cataloging-in-Publication Data

Names: Hurd, Ian, author.
Title: How to do things with international law / Ian Hurd.
Description: Princeton, New Jersey : Princeton University Press, 2017. | Includes
bibliographical references and index.
Identifiers: LCCN 2017019523 | ISBN 9780691170114 (hardback)
Subjects: LCSH: International law. | Rule of law. | BISAC: POLITICAL SCIENCE /
International Relations / Treaties. | LAW / International. | POLITICAL SCIENCE /
Government / International.
Classification: LCC KZ3410 .H87 2017 | DDC 341—dc23 LC record available at https://
lccn.loc.gov/2017019523

British Library Cataloging-in-Publication Data is available

This book has been composed in Adobe Text Pro and Gotham

Printed on acid-free paper. ∞

Printed in the United States of America

10 9 8 7 6 5 4 3 2 1

HOW TO DO THINGS WITH INTERNATIONAL LAW

CONTENTS

ACKNOWLEDGMENTS

This book explores the politics of international law. It examines a series of recent controversies in international affairs, and draws out their legal and political threads in order to think about the political powers of international law. I do not seek to account for all corners of international law, or give a prescriptive case for what should or shouldn't be done. Those in search of an answer to the question of whether to be for or against international law may be disappointed. Instead, the book focuses on international law as political practice.

I have been thinking about the law and politics of international affairs for some time in conversation with numerous friends, colleagues, and contributors to the field. I am particularly grateful to Robert Howse, Jens David Ohlin, Jennifer Mitzen, Frédéric Mégret, Elizabeth Shakman Hurd, Jutta Brunnée, Nisha Fazal, Mary Ellen O'Connell, Karen Alter, Nicholas Rengger, Antje Weiner, Anthony Lang, Michael Barnett, Mara Pillinger, Jean-Marc Coicaud, Vincent Pouliot, Mikael Rask Madsen, Michael Zürn, Helen Kinsella, Shirley Scott, Nikolas Rajkovic, Ingo Venzke, Scott Veitch, G. John Ikenberry, Anne-Marie Slaughter, Martha Finnemore, Chris Reus-Smit, Andreas Føllesdal, Terry Halliday, Jothie Rajah, Charlotte Epstein, Philippe Sands, Greg Shaffer, Michael Byers, José Alvarez, Ian Johnstone, Jacob Katz Cogan, Carne Ross, and Rosa Brooks.

I became interested in the international rule of law and its politics during a sabbatical year at the Woodrow Wilson School at Princeton University in 2010. I thank Helen Milner and the Niehaus program for making that possible. I enjoyed short stays at WZB (the Berlin Social Science Center) in 2012 and EHESS in Paris in 2013, both of which were helpful in the early formulation of the book. I'm grateful to Michael Zürn at WZB and Liora Israël at EHESS and their colleagues. The book was finished in 2016–17, which I spent as a visiting scholar at the American Bar Foundation. Terry Halliday, Jothie Rajah, and Ajay Mehrotra and their colleagues make the foundation an ideal environment for thinking about the practical life of law and legalization. I appreciate as well the many audiences and panels that have listened to parts of this project; this book would not exist without their helpful input.

Throughout my work, Northwestern University has been a friendly home. In addition to the support of the political science department, I am grateful to the Buffett Institute for Global Studies. I have benefited in countless ways from the intellectual community and professional opportunities that the Buffett Institute sustains. Its Working Group on International Organization and International Law is a long-running forum for research on politics and law in international affairs. The Equality Development and Globalization Studies group at Buffett supported a book workshop at which Jennifer Mitzen, Jens David Ohlin, Rob Howse, and Fred Mégret gave their time and energy to this project.

I have been lucky to work with engaging and thoughtful graduate students at Northwestern. In the closing stages of this project, I benefited particularly from conversations with Erin Lockwood, Swati Srivastava, Sidra Hamidi, Josh Freedman, Ceyda Erten, and Lena Trabucco.

The final manuscript was greatly improved by the close editorial attention of Simon Waxman. Cindy Milstein did a terrific job of copyediting. I appreciate also the contributions of Eric Crahan, my editor at Princeton University Press, and Chuck Myers, his predecessor there, for their input as the project advanced.

My most important debt in this, as in everything else, is to Beth, Ally, Sophie, and Audrey. I am lucky to be on this adventure with them.

The following publishers have given permission to reprint sections from previously published work.

Parts of chapter 2 appeared in "The International Rule of Law and the Domestic Analogy," *Global Constitutionalism* 45, no. 3 (2015): 365–95.

A version of chapter 4 appeared as "The Permissive Power of the Ban on War," *European Journal of International Security* 2, no. 1 (2016): 1–18.

Material from chapter 6 appeared in "Torture and the Politics of Legitimation in International Law," in *The Legitimacy of International Human Rights Regimes: Legal, Political, and Philosophical Perspectives*, ed. Andreas Føllesdal, Johan Karlsson Schaffer, and Geir Ulfstein (Cambridge: Cambridge University Press, 2013), 165–89.

1

Introduction

—*Well what would you do if you were the king? asked the prince.*
—*I would do absolutely nothing*
—*And who then would govern?*
—*The Laws!*

—FRANÇOIS QUESNAY TO THE DAUPHIN, CITED IN BERNARD
HARCOURT, *THE ILLUSION OF FREE MARKETS*

Aerial drones, humanitarian intervention, cyberattacks, torture.
The big debates in world politics today are inseparable from international law. Controversy over what is and is not legal is standard fare in international conflicts, and commitment to rule of law
is presumed a marker of good governance. Rule following is said
to lead naturally to more desirable collective outcomes.

This *legalization* of global affairs is widely viewed as a progressive advance on earlier conditions. No longer must self-interest,
coercion, and power politics dominate decision making. Now the
rule of law is cited as the remedy for human rights abuses, domestic
dictatorship, international war, and other problems.[1] For instance,
as Anne-Marie Slaughter says, it is "far better to resolve boundary

issues in the South China Sea multilaterally by agreed-upon rules of the game than unilaterally by the strongest nation."[2] Along with scholars, governments, activists, and nongovernmental organizations (NGOs) routinely emphasize the significance of international law and urge states and nonstate actors alike to conform to its requirements. The United Nations recently established a bureau to promote and coordinate its rule-of-law activities internally and around the world.[3] The Pentagon opened its Office for Rule of Law and International Humanitarian Policy in 2010. In these efforts, the rule of law appears as a charmed concept, outside politics, without doubters and without critics. Keally McBride says it is treated "as a largely uncontested self-evident good."[4] As Quesnay said to the dauphin, let the laws themselves rule. Yet the politics of the international rule of law are not so simple and are rarely investigated directly.[5]

In this book, I look at how the concept is used in world politics and to what ends. My goal is to better understand the power and politics of international law.[6] I show that international law is properly seen not as a set of rules external to and constraining of state power but rather as a social practice in which states and others engage. They put the political power of international law to work in the pursuit of their goals and interests.

Governments use international law to explain and justify their choices. This is both constraining and permissive. On the one hand, states must fit their preferences into legal forms. On the other hand, they are empowered when they can show their choices to be lawful. Thus international law makes it easier for states to do some things (those that can be presented as lawful) and harder to do others (those that appear to be unlawful).

The legalization of politics is permissive even as it imposes limits. States strive to fit their policies into the categories of international law, showing themselves to be compliant with their obligations. But in doing so, they appear to depoliticize their choices. Compliance with the law becomes the marker for acceptable policy, masking the substantive politics of the situation and the law itself.

This is not to say that law never limits state power. It can be a source of individual emancipation and a bulwark of human rights. Beth Simmons reflects this conventional view when she says, "It is precisely because of their potential power to constrain that treaty commitments are contentious in domestic and international politics."[7] But it is not necessarily so. Against the "enchanted" view of law as naturally progressive and protective against state power, I suggest we adopt a more empirical attitude in which law's normative valence is a question for investigation rather than assumed in advance. Drawing on several case studies, I will argue that attention to the actual content of international law as well as its application and interpretation demands new conclusions about law's political implications. We cannot get away with assumptions of inherently superior, apolitical rule following.

In part this is because the rules themselves mutate according to political exigency. If law were above politics, it would be easy to distinguish between the legality and illegality of foreign policy choices. But, in the cases I examine, international law does a notably poor job of differentiating compliance from violation. For instance, despite decades of debates, it remains unclear just what kinds of force may be justified under the laws of self-defense. Even the general parameters of self-defense have changed over the years with shifting circumstances—specifically, as powerful states come to need or desire new legitimations for new forms of war in relation to new forms of threat.[8] In other words, the contents of the law change through its use. I also find that international law is often much more successful at constituting and legitimating government policies than at positively distinguishing between compliance and noncompliance. The international rule of law is thus a permissive regime as much as a constraining one, and its relationship to power is more complicated than standard assumptions acknowledge.

The International Rule of Law and Its Politics

In 1908, Lassa Oppenheim looked forward to the day that historians would declare the "ultimate victory of international law over international anarchy."[9] According to many liberal internationalists, the international rule of law brings us closer to that day. G. John Ikenberry says we live in a "rules-based international order."[10] John H. Jackson, the eminent international trade lawyer and scholar, takes this view to the extreme when he says, "To a large degree the history of civilization may be described as a gradual evolution from a power-oriented approach, in the state of nature, to a rule-oriented approach."[11] It is a good thing, too, according to President Dwight David Eisenhower. Faced with the threat of nuclear proliferation, Eisenhower propounded the liberal perspective in which law is an *alternative* to power: "In a very real sense the world no longer has a choice between force and law. If civilization is to survive, it must choose the rule of law."[12] Compliance with law is equated with political order, stability, and peaceful settlement of disputes, while failures to abide by the rule of law are said to provide the raw materials for innumerable international crises.

In this account, law is a counterpoint to power. Obligation to comply with law binds governments acting internationally in much the same way law binds individuals within states. Through law, governments escape a global Lockean state of nature: agents recognize their weakness and the dangers of anarchy and so consent to limits on their absolute freedom, thereby establishing a political system that better serves their individual and collective needs.[13]

The domestic model of law and legal obligation, however, does not translate well to the international realm. The conventional account of international law, based in this model, both overstates and understates the power of the rule of law in international affairs. It overstates because states do not automatically and unproblematically comply with international law, as individuals generally do with respect to domestic law. Governments frequently break, ignore, avoid, and redefine their international legal obligations. Thus, as many have noted, the regulative capacity of international law is weak.[14] Moreover, many of the most important rules of international law permit fundamentally conflicting interpretations. As a result, it may not be possible to identify clearly what compliance means in order to assess rule following versus rule breaking.

At the same time, the conventional view understates the power of international law because it begins with the assumption that the power of law rests in its capacity to limit strong actors. If law can't constrain the powerful, it is said, then it is probably not doing its job.[15] But the focus on constraint is misplaced. It rests on a narrow conception of law and legalization along with an unrealistic ideal-type view of law's relation to politics. Law has power to constrain, but it also has powers to authorize, permit, and constitute actions. Legal realists of various types and constructivists in international relations (IR) emphasize these powers.[16] As I show in the following chapters, the instrumental use of law to legitimize state policy is ubiquitous.[17] For instance, law is used in public diplomacy to explain and frame competing policy choices, and as such, offers resources states rely on.[18] In this sense, international law is pervasive and even foundational in global affairs. It shapes the context in which governments operate and provides the raw materials with which foreign policy is pursued.

In practice, international rules provoke two kinds of interpretation, which complicates their meaning. Participants in international law interpret rules in order to provide an account of what actions are allowed or forbidden, and they interpret the case at hand in order to know how it fits with those rules. It is therefore hard to establish clean boundaries among states, their interests, and the meaning of international rules. These processes are also open to nonstate actors, and while I do not focus on them here, it is apparent that much of the politics of international law happens in a broader public domain, beyond formal state or legal settings.

For example, the NGO Sea Shepherd says it is enforcing the International Convention on the Regulation of Whaling when it interrupts Japanese whale hunting in the southern ocean.[19] Similarly, the Institute for Development and Justice in Haiti, a US NGO, claims its efforts to gain compensation for cholera victims in Haiti are authorized by the Status of Forces Agreement between the United Nations and Haitian government.[20] The various parties to international law, whether states or otherwise, are constantly rewriting the rules as a function of their deployment.

Scope and Goals of the Book

The idea that state behavior should be consistent with international law is deeply rooted in international law and politics, both in practice and scholarship. This demand for compliance constitutes the ideology of the rule of law and carries important consequences for the conduct of international affairs.[21] Among these is the political legitimation that comes from being seen as compliant with international law. This is attractive to states. On the flip side, international actors can undermine others' power by showing that they are violating the law. What I've sketched here is a political understanding of law by which I mean the recognition that law produces both winners and losers. States and rules are mutually implicating, law and politics inseparable. This leads away from the conventional view in at least three ways.

First, my understanding avoids much of the debate about the "true" meaning of international legal rules. This is a major concern among theorists and observers of international law. The ability to differentiate compliance and noncompliance is often taken to be the hallmark of a well-functioning legal system; the rule of law itself is usually said to require that actors be able to distinguish what is legal from what is not, and international law is frequently faulted for its inadequacy on this point, particularly for the lack of a judicial branch with automatic jurisdiction over interstate disputes. To remedy this apparent problem, scholars and others invest in codification, the "rational design" of international institutions, and other projects that aim to clarify the meaning of existing laws or institute better ones.[22] Relatedly, much social science scholarship on international law asks whether the law induces states to change their behavior, from noncompliance to compliance.[23] This is consistent with the tradition of positivism as a research method: positivists look for the causal impact of an independent variable (international law) on a dependent variable (state behavior). Both positivist social science and rational design require that the law be separate from and prior to the behavior it governs.

In the chapters that follow, a stable notion of compliance is elusive, at least with respect to a large subset of important international legal obligations. So there can be no comparison between law and practice. Contestation over the meaning and application of law is endemic to law's political uses and effects. Indeed, compliance may be a political rather than legal artifact— the thing being contested as opposed to an external standard that can be applied to behavior. To assess an actor's compliance with international law involves more than reading formal sources of law. It also entails the rendering of political judgment about what policies deserve to be endorsed. Put another way, international law cannot be separated from state practice, and state practice does not exist independent of the legal explanations, justifications, and rationalizations that governments give for it. Debates about the true meaning of international rules therefore are bound to be inconclusive. If we are to understand what international law is and is used for, we need a research methodology attentive to the mutual constitution of states and rules.

Second, I depart from conventional readings of international law by highlighting the dialectical relationship between state policies and international rules. It is not just that the meaning of international law shifts under the influence of state practice. The relationship between state interests and international rules is bidirectional and mutually constituting. Governments rely on international law to construct their foreign policies and in so doing contribute to remaking those rules. State practice is jurisgenerative of international law: it creates the resources that constitute it.

For instance, the debate over whether the US drone program is legal or not depends on how states have in the past given meaning to various legal categories and concepts, including interstate war, the Geneva Conventions and other instruments, the legal personality of nonstate actors, and command responsibility.

When states use the legal resources of the international system to explain or justify their actions, they change how those resources are understood for purposes of future cases and thereby refashion the law in ways that influence policy choices.[24] Thus the categories of "lawful" and "unlawful" are closely related to states' interests, desires, and past and present choices. The distinction between legality and illegality, on which positivist accounts of international law rest, is both an output of state practice and an input to it.

This point has substantive and methodological implications. Substantively, it means that we should not treat states' references to international law as easy rhetoric or cheap talk. To do so overlooks the investment in law and legal language: states feel pressure to frame their actions as rule abiding and consistent with their legal obligations. When they do so, they can reap political benefits. Couching actions in law is not the same as complying with law, but this does not mean that compliance is irrelevant. My point is that what it means to comply, to act consistently with one's obligations, is the currency of contestation in the politics of international law.

Scholars have recognized international law's susceptibility to manipulation but often draw from this overly narrow conclusions. For instance Stephen Krasner shows that leaders use the rules of state sovereignty to strengthen their claims on power but argues that this instrumental manipulation signals the weakness of those rules.[25] Yet we might instead say that there is productive power in the rhetorical use of these rules. Openness to this possibility is the beginning of inquiry into how such power works and what it yields.

From the standpoint of methodology, the mutual constitution of states and rules means the two cannot be isolated and treated as distinct variables. State interests are not independent of the legal resources in the international system, and legal resources are not independent of state interests. To understand how international law works, then, we must employ new research approaches attentive to its use rather than ideal theories of what law is.

The third novel contribution of this book follows from the previous two. By bringing together political power and international law, I address some of the problems that arise when they are kept apart. This forced separation conditions international politics— and the study thereof—in at least three important ways. First, under the regime of separation, states are asked to prioritize between their self-interests and the communal position, where the former is unstructured by law and the latter is law defined.[26] Second, IR theory then divides between realists—who a priori expect the nonlaw position to prevail—and liberals—who believe that well-crafted law suits the mutual interests of states and may therefore hold sway in certain circumstances.[27] Finally, separation tends to elevate law's standing because law is thought to closely model morality and foster collective progress, while power and politics are associated with coercion, disorder, and unilateralism.[28]

This book shows that international law and international power cannot be separated, and in doing so, rejects the assumed opposition between the two. Where scholars in the liberal tradition celebrate international law for its capacity to protect human welfare against state power, I argue that lawfulness confers political legitimation and may or may not limit states' power and flexibility. Law itself has no preference for human welfare. The legalization of international politics may reduce coercion and destruction, and it may strengthen states' ability to make war or deploy drones.

This malleability reflects the sources of international rules and patterns of rule following. Rules are constructed through negotiation among motivated actors seeking to shape the legal landscape to suit their interests. Powerful actors presumably have more success in these negotiations than do weaker ones. Once rules are in place, agents try to bring them to bear on disputes and policies in ways that, again, suit their interests. Here, too, state power is in play. Strong states can more easily shoulder the costs of international rule breaking than can weaker states, as the United States showed in the Iraq invasion of 2003. And when strong states break rules, their choices may be taken as evidence of a change in the rules. Rule breaking by weak states is less likely to have such effect.[29]

Accepting that international law is a function of political power does not mean adopting the perspective of IR realists. To see why, we must get a handle on just what realists believe. For some IR scholars, anyone attentive to differences in the use of power is a realist.[30] This is misleading. Realism does not have a monopoly on the study of international power politics; indeed, most approaches to IR, from realist to constructivist to Marxist to critical theory and more, are interested in power.

What distinguishes IR realism is its particularly narrow conceptualization of power in terms of military and industrial capacity.[31] Thus realism's characteristic concern with comparative access to military hardware. For realists, fighting capacity is distinct from, and more important than, power found in law, morals, ideas, concepts, or identities. By contrast, other approaches see these as sources or expressions of power. For instance, Benno Teschke, arguing for a wider conception of power, sees state sovereignty itself as a function of the power of international capital and demands of the capital-controlling class.[32] Charlotte Epstein examines power mobilized in the 1970s through the rising antiwhaling discourse, which had profound consequences for the legal regime of the International Whaling Commission.[33] Andrew Guzman sees reputation as a form of power among states, a kind of currency with its own economy. The desire to cultivate a good reputation induces states to take certain actions and refrain from others even when they perceive benefits from acting differently.[34]

In all these cases, international law is at once a potential constraint on the power of states, a tool with which states can increase their power over others, and a by-product of some actors' power. It is thoroughly implicated in power politics. In sum, that international law is politically useful does not demonstrate the triumph of realist "Machiavellian parochialists."[35]

The usefulness of international law is acknowledged in the concept of *lawfare*, the strategy or tactic of using international law to pursue goals.[36] The term has come to be associated with *abuse*: in an unwelcome development, weak states illegitimately use international law to constrain the strong.[37] But it is a mistake to identify lawfare as an aberration or solely a weapon of the weak. Lawfare is better seen as the typical condition of international law. Indeed, law is more likely to serve as a tool of the strong than of the weak, since it is the strong who have the greatest influence over the design of international rules and the greatest capacity to both deploy and evade them. This is evident in US liberal internationalists' enthusiasm for international law. Many see international institutions and law as protecting US interests and hope that other states will accede to the existing rules rather than attempt to rewrite them.[38]

The chapters that follow explore these themes in detail. I show that states remake international law as they use it to pursue their interests. Those states are simultaneously bound and empowered. Practice, legality, and state interests are mutually implicated, and the international rule of law is the institution that emerges from their repeated interaction. Indeed, the strategic use of international law *is* international law.

The International Rule of Law in Practice: Cases and Chapters

The conventional perspective on the international rule of law is Lockean: law amounts to "externally imposed obligatory constraints"—freestanding rules and institutions that exercise authority over states.[39] In chapters 2 and 3, I explain my alternative view. I then document it in chapters 4 through 6, focusing on cases demonstrating law's capacity to enable, permit, and constitute state action.

Chapter 2 looks at the domestic rule of law and its uneasy trans-
lation to international politics. The central claim is this: the domestic rule of law is in effect when there exists a set of stable public
laws binding in theory and practice on both citizens and the state.
As Rosa Brooks puts it, "At root it's pretty simple. The rule of law
requires that governments follow transparent, universally applicable, and clearly defined laws and procedures."[40] From this broad
notion come disagreements about the content and nature of the
rules and their effects.

There are two main lines of debate in existing literature on the
domestic rule of law. The first asks whether individual human
rights and collective social welfare are effects of the rule of law or
constitutive of it. This produces a distinction between formalist
and substantive theories of the rule of law. The second debate
involves how the rule *of* law can be distinguished from rule *by* law,
in which the state uses the framework of law instrumentally to
legitimate and reinforce its domination.

Three claims about the rule of law are constant across these
debates: that rules should be public and stable, that rules should
apply to the government as well as the citizens, and that the rules
should be applied equally across cases. None of these translates
easily to the realm of international law. I therefore argue that domestic rule of law provides an unsuitable model for an international equivalent.

Drawing on legal realism and practice theory in IR, chapter 3
presents an account of the international rule of law that reflects
the particular dynamics of international politics. On this reading,
the international rule of law is a social practice that states and
others engage in when they provide legal reasons and justifications
for their actions. The goal may be either political legitimation for
oneself or delegitimation of adversaries. This sort of use of international law both relies on and reinforces the idea that states
should act lawfully rather than unlawfully. The priority of lawfulness is taken for granted.

The approach I outline in chapter 3 helps to make sense of international law's contribution to contemporary disputes and crises. In chapters 4, 5, and 6, I examine the relationship between international law and war, torture, and drones. Each is a highly legalized corner of international politics. Governments expend considerable effort to present their positions as consistent with international law and characterize their opponents as violators. International legal instruments, from the Charter of the United Nations to multilateral treaties, largely provide the terms of debate. Despite—or perhaps because of—this high degree of legalization, what constitutes compliance with international law is contested and perhaps unresolvable.

In the disputes I examine, all players profess their commitment to the rule of law and their intent to fulfill specific international legal obligations. But the distinction between legality and illegality in these cases is more political construction than legal fact. Determination of lawfulness follows use of international law rather than preceding it.[41] Moreover, in each dispute the protagonists provide legal interpretations motivated by the desire to legitimize their actions through law. Thus the teleology of their legal reasoning points toward their own interest, and state practice shapes the content of international law toward the preferences of strong states.

The meanings of key legal terms in these disputes are neither self-evident nor matters of consensus. In the course of the disputes themselves, the legal terms are interpreted by various parties, always in ways that are informed by their interests. To explore this, I follow methods similar to those Bernard Harcourt, Helen Kinsella, and others use to study category distinctions in other settings. In *The Illusion of Free Markets*, Harcourt looks at the social construction of the divide between free markets and government regulation.[42] Kinsella, in *The Image before the Weapon*, focuses on the differentiation of civilians and combatants in the laws of war.[43] As with legality and illegality, these distinctions are made instead of found. They rely, as Kinsella says, on "an established rather than an inherent contrast," yet they carry significant political consequences in the world.[44]

To see the difference between established and inherent contrast, consider the US use of drones in war against terrorists and other kinds of enemies. Is it legal? The conventional approach to international law suggests that US policy makers should consult written conventions to determine under what circumstances the use of drones is legal, then decide whether the current circumstances suit that definition, and finally make a choice informed by this consultation.[45] They may decide to cross the line into illegality; the standard model does not predict that they will comply with the law, only that the law will help organize foreign policy choices into legal and illegal options.

Missing from this process is the connection between law and politics, and therefore the controversy inherent in the matter. The legality of today's drone warfare is controversial because it is not clear which legal resources are relevant to the practice and because the choice of resources is inseparable from one's position on the desirability of the activity itself.

When we take stock of the underlying legal questions, it becomes clear that the answers have significant political implications. Are drones like conventional aircraft bombers and so governed by preexisting rules concerning the dropping of bombs in times of war? If so, the questions relevant to legality include the belligerent status of the United States and the state where the drone is operating; the *jus in bello* rules of proportionality, distinction, and necessity; and more. Then there is the further question of whether the current situation is a war in the international legal sense, and if so, between whom? Or are drone killings more like political assassinations? In that case, the laws of war are irrelevant. Do the people targeted for killing by drones share a corporate identity with the people who organized the 9/11 attacks? If they do, then killing them may represent a lawful use of force in self-defense under the UN Charter and the Authorization for Use of Military

Force in US law.[46] Do due process rules apply? Do the targeted individuals have rights, and if so, of what kind and in which jurisdiction?

Deciding whether the United States is complying with international law requires answering these questions and more, but the choice of questions themselves is a matter of political determination. So the legality of the conduct can be assessed only after rounds of political interpretation. Policy makers, scholars, and military officials are equally at sea when it comes to understanding how to apply international law to drones, with the result that the generic policy commitment to comply with international law has little content.

Despite this, US officials have sought a legal framing in which drone killings appear lawful. This suggests politics at work: the politics of international law require that the United States provide a legal defense of its drone policy even where there exists no coherent body of law to appeal to. And the outcome of this political work, so far, indicates law's permissiveness. Choices about which law is relevant are motivated by the consequences they generate for the legality of the policy itself: critics of the drone program ask legal questions that lead to a finding of illegality, while drone enthusiasts ask legal questions that produce the opposite result.

It is tempting to assume that the ambiguity surrounding the legality of drone-based killing—and the exploitation of that ambiguity—is a function of drones' novelty. But the problem is not that drones are a new technology. The political utility of legal justification is not limited to novel policy questions. The political productivity of law exists by virtue of legalization itself—in the fact that legal resources are used to legitimate and delegitimate political conditions or decisions.[47] This is true whether or not the contested behavior is well established.

To illustrate this, chapter 4 examines a classical area of international law: the use of force by states. The ban on war is often cited as the centerpiece of the modern international legal-political system and used to distinguish the contemporary age from earlier, less legalized periods.[48] Liberal convention sees the ban on war as a legal constraint on states' political choices; states seeking to uphold the international rule of are advised to refrain from using force against other states.

But this understanding is flawed. The UN Charter outlaws some kinds of war and permits others, such as those undertaken in self-defense. I show that the Charter is a mechanism by which law sorts the motivations for war into lawful (self-defense) and unlawful (all others) categories. It thereby creates a framework to legitimate wars and reduce their political costs. The Charter is not antiwar: it is explicitly permissive of war so long as the claimed motive is self-defense.

Chapter 4 also charts how the law has changed since 1945 in response to changing state practice. In particular, the understanding of what is permitted and forbidden by the self-defense exemption contained in Articles 2(4) and 51 of the Charter has shifted. As the perceived dangers in the international system have changed, states have changed the rules so that they can use force without leaving the confines of legal behavior. The definition of legal use of force thus internalizes states interests in two distinct ways: first, because states are permitted to use force in response to perceived threats originating in other states; second, because post-1945 interpretative practice has removed the limits of time and space implied in Article 51 of the Charter. The ban on war after 1945 has produced a legalized version of the nineteenth-century rationale for war: raisons d'état supported by legal justifications.

Chapter 5 explores the legality of latter-day weapons—specifically, nuclear arms and lethal drones—to consider the potential for voids in the coverage of international law. When technological or other developments enable previously inconceivable kinds of warfare, states face open legal questions. Recent debates over the legality of US drones illustrate this, as do earlier debates about the legality of nuclear arms. The weapons arise in a kind of legal vacuum, empty of specific regulation. Drawing on these examples, I consider the power of the international rule of law in situations where there may be no law.

With respect to nuclear weapons, the International Court of Justice decided that despite there being no directly applicable laws, use is nonetheless governed by international law. Rules designed for other weapons are relevant, as is a general principle that in the end, international law must defend states' rights to protect their national security as they see fit. These two sets of resources— general principles and analogies to other laws—are also important in legal debates over drones today: the lawfulness of drones as instruments of war is inferred from the legality of what are said to be analogous weapons from earlier times, and the needs of the state are internalized in legality debates through the mechanism of self-defense. The perception of threat justifies the legality of the military action, in a self-fulfilling circle of interiorization.

These debates reveal the inescapability of international law: it fills legal dead zones, as if under the influence of a horror vacui. Even a new policy, one for which treaties and custom have not yet been created, is seen as already structured by international law. The prelegalization condition, which presumably exists before law is written and on which much of the legalization literature in IR depends, does not exist. Law-free policy space is impossible.

The legal status of torture is the subject of chapter 6, where I examine the implications of an international ban on torture that coexists with a nontrivial level of torture in practice. This is not simply a case of torture law being violated. There is wide, perhaps- unanimous, agreement that torture is prohibited by international law, and the legitimacy of the ban is rarely contested. The rule is established most directly by the Geneva Conventions and 1984 Convention against Torture and Other Cruel, Inhuman, or De- grading Treatment (CAT), but it is also widely held that torture is outlawed under *jus cogens* norms intrinsic in the international system.[49]

Despite this, many governments engage in practices that seem clearly prohibited by laws against torture. Much of this behavior comes with detailed defense of its legality. Thus the politics of torture generally address questions of what constitutes torture, not concerns over the ban itself. The connection between law and behavior does not fit neatly into categories of compliance and violation, and the politics overflow the bounds of these positivist legal containers. For example, the US government in the 2000s encased its use of torture in an extensive legal framework drawn from international sources including the CAT. International lawyers, largely unconvinced, disputed the contention that US torture was lawful.[50] But the fact that the US government attempted to justify its behavior using legal resources designed to forbid torture speaks to the political power of international law. Such efforts illustrate what Scott Veitch calls law's capacity to define "irresponsibility"— that is, law can define an actor as not responsible for the harms it has caused.[51] This is precisely how Bush administration used antitorture law: to demonstrate that its actions were not subject to the rules. Officials sought a zone of legally protected irresponsibility. They used international law against torture as tools to legalize torture.

Each of the cases detailed in this book shows different aspects of the relationship between international law and world politics, but all serve the same goal: to illuminate the international rule of law as it actually exists. On the basis of this history, I conclude in chapter 7 that the international rule of law is a structure of political authority. It creates a hierarchy in international affairs in which legal obligations are superior and governments are subordinate. The structure depends on and is reinforced by the widespread practice of legal justification by states. Within that structure, international law is at once constraining, empowering, and constituting of the foreign policies of governments. I use the language of "empire" to describe this structure. It is a centralized and hierarchical system that unites its subjects under a single political authority, the empire of international legalism.

2

The Rule of Law, Domestic and International

At the end of the day the rule of law must prevail.
—DAVID SCHEFFER, INTERVIEW WITH DAVID BOSCO
FOR THE *MULTILATERALIST*

The rule of law is a concept that originates in domestic law and politics, and has been transplanted to explain and argue for international governance. This chapter examines this transition and some problems it raises. I first lay out the components that are commonly included in the domestic rule of law and then show the difficulties in carrying these into the domain of global governance. Each of the key components of the domestic rule of law is contradicted by something important in the international legal/political context. In reaction to this, the international version of the rule of law is often defined instead with the idea of compliance at its core: the expectation that states should comply with their legal obligations. This escapes the problems of the domestic analogy, but leads to a notion of legalization that misses much of the political contribution of law to international affairs. The discussion in this chapter then sets up chapter 3, which shows that the practice of international law in fact contradicts the compliance model, and suggests instead that the international rule of law exists in the dynamic between international legal resources and political instrumentalism. The subsequent empirical chapters explore this in practice around contemporary legal and political disputes.

The rule of law is central to both the conception of the modern state as well as the study of international law and world politics. It is problematic and controversial in both areas, though for different reasons. The domestic and international versions of the rule of law are different in light of the different political arrangements they are meant to govern; each is a response to a different set of historical challenges and is a solution to a different set of problems. The domestic rule of law is rooted in struggles between citizens and governments over the use and misuse of state power. It is meant to place limits on the exercise of state authority and create a stable set of known rules that apply equally to all citizens.

The international rule of law, by contrast, deals with legally autonomous states whose interdependence creates both positive and negative externalities. In IR, with ostensibly no formal hierarchy or governance structure, sovereign states have the capacity to tailor their legal obligations largely as they wish. The agency every state possesses means that each can have a unique portfolio of legal obligations, produced by its past commitments and actions in relation to various treaties, customary rules, and interpretative positions.[1] These commitments constitute a rule-of-law international order to the extent that states accept the binding nature of international treaties and other obligations. This requires a fundamentally different model of the rule of law than is found in domestic legal and social theory.

Some essential elements of the domestic rule of law (for instance, a certain kind of control over political authority) do not translate well to the international setting. But others, such as the legitimacy of transferring obligations via consent, are better suited to the international rather than domestic realm—international actors (that is, states) make explicit acts of consent to binding legal instruments, while domestic social contract theory has endless trouble specifying how or when individuals give consent to their state. Despite these differences, the two versions are united by a common set of commitments: the rule of law is seen as an alternative to the arbitrary exercise of power; the outcome of a rule-of-law system is the choice by the law's subjects to *comply* with the rules; and these choices naturally generate valuable goods that are threatened or undersupplied in the absence of the rule of law. The limitations of these commitments are evident in the chapters that follow.

In this chapter, I begin with a version of the concept as used in domestic settings and identify three components generally thought to be integral to the rule of law. Each of the three is problematic when applied to the international variant, and so in its second section, the chapter turns to consider how the rule of law has been reconceptualized for international law and politics. This centers on the notion of the obligation to comply, which in turn presumes an unrealistic clarity and stability of legal resources. The practical uses of international law in fact do not depend on agreement over the meaning of compliance, and so in chapter 3 I advance a practice-theory version of international legal politics.

The Domestic Theory of the Rule of Law

The rule of law is a form of social order, a mode of organizing the relationships of authority that exist among potentially competing social institutions including legal institutions, government, leaders, and citizens. It refers to a social system in which stable rules exist that are binding on the citizens and government alike, with the overall objective to "prevent the misuse and abuse of political power."[2] This can be understood and institutionalized in a variety of ways, leading to vigorous debates in political philosophy, sociology, legal theory, and comparative politics about what it is, and where it exists or doesn't.[3]

From these debates, a conventional core is often identified that centers on three essential requirements:

- society should be governed by stable, public, and certain rules

- these rules should apply equally to the governed and to the rulers
- these rules should be applied equally and dispassionately across cases and people

These three appear in various ways in the scholarship of legal philosophers. Brian Tamanaha labels them "formal legality," "government limited by law," and "rule of law, not man."[4] Simon Chesterman, following A. V. Dicey, sees the three as "regulating government power, implying equality before the law, and privileging judicial process."[5] Lon Fuller expands his list to eight principles of the "internal morality of law."[6] The World Justice Project Rule of Law Index sees them as four.[7] The differences are minor because there is a great deal of overlap in the core propositions: stable public rules, which are applied equally among citizens, and equally between citizens and the government. The three components are more than procedural requirements; they require a substantive commitment to dividing political power in a certain way. But they fall short of constituting a full theory of society because they provide only a framework in which other goals are pursued, not the goals themselves. I examine each in its domestic setting before turning to how they do or do not translate to the interstate context.

PUBLIC, STABLE RULES

Formal legality describes the sense in which rules must be made such that individuals can distinguish between legal and illegal actions. The rules must be clear and public, forward-looking, and written in language that is sufficiently specific and yet designed for general categories of behavior rather than particular incidents. A functionalist case for formal legality rests on the argument that law can only be a useful guide for individual behavior if the citizen can be reasonably confident that they know what is lawful and what is not. Unless the rules are public, prospective, and somewhat stable, the citizen cannot meaningfully take them into account when acting. As Joseph Raz says, "The law should be such that people will be able to be guided by it. . . . The law must be capable of being obeyed. . . . It must be such that they can find out what it is and act on it."[8] This underpins Friedrich Hayek's point that predictability in the law is essential for its contribution to human liberty.[9] The ability to differentiate the lawful from the unlawful undergirds the law's capacity to influence decisions, organize society, and predict general patterns of mass behavior.

The goal of fixed and known rules is in perpetual tension with the possibility of making changes in the law. Law should be stable but also open to change and amendment—thus, for instance, when Raz discusses the stability of the law, he couches it as *"relative"* stability.[10] This is managed in the theory of the rule of law by constructing nontrivial institutional requirements that govern the process for changing laws—parliamentary approval, for example, or a plebiscite. These are distinct from rules designed to prevent the government from taking certain substantive decisions, as might be controlled by a constitution or bill of rights that makes it impossible for the state to seek certain ends. The procedural rules on lawmaking make it more difficult for the state to change existing law but they must not make it impossible. Of course, this generates the real danger that the capacity of the government to change the law will undo the benefits thought to come from relatively stable law in the first place, and as a consequence, leads to the second component of the rule of law: subordination of the government itself to the body of law.

GOVERNMENT LIMITED BY LAWS

The knowability and stability of the law are not enough for the rule of law. The doctrine of the rule of law also insists on certain forms of equality. One of these is represented by what Tamanaha calls government limited by law, which is the requirement "the state and its officials are limited by the law" just as are regular citizens.[11] (The second is described below as equality of application across cases.) The law is binding on all citizens, and all operate in the context of the law. In Dicey's words, this means "not only that with us no man is above the law, but . . . that here, every man, whatever be his rank or condition, is subject to the ordinary law of the realm and amenable to the jurisdiction of the ordinary tribunals."[12] This is the idea at the heart of Karen Alter's suggestion that "diminishing the absolute power of governments is, of course, the objective of the rule of law."[13] This provision subordinates the government to the law, and equalizes individuals and government as subjects of the law. Its absence in a legal system is often described as "rule by law," in which "authoritarian rulers . . . capitalize on the regime-supporting roles that courts perform while minimizing their utility to the political opposition."[14] As we will see below, the application of this aspect of the rule of law to the international context is problematic due to the different nature of governance in the interstate realm.

RULES APPLIED CONSISTENTLY ACROSS CASES

Finally, the rule of law requires that the law be applied across cases in a particular manner—that judges and government officials follow or apply the relevant body of rules to the situation before them in accordance with laws or norms of procedure.[15] This is usually seen as being in distinction to the arbitrary exercise of power of some individuals over others, or decisions taken based on the particular character or identity of the parties. As Raz has noted, this does not prevent laws that treat different groups or people unequally—such as guaranteeing rights to landowners that are not given to others.[16] Inequalities created by law are common and perhaps inevitable.[17] The rule of law requires only that the terms and categories created by law be applied equally across the cases to which they apply. This element of the concept produces the independent judiciary. Courts, "with the duty of applying the law to cases brought before them and whose judgments and conclusions as to the legal merits of those cases are final," are one device to implement the dispassionate adjudication of disputes arising in and from law.[18] Other institutions may well serve this purpose, too, or instead, but the independent judiciary is its leading institutional form in domestic societies today.

These three elements combine to constitute the conventional account of the rule of law and show that the rule of law is an amalgamated concept.[19] Its various components represent answers to different political problems and come from distinct historical processes of contestation.[20] These can be combined in different ways, giving rise to the comparative study of legal systems within the rule-of-law family. They are nevertheless usually seen as mutually reinforcing, and constituting together a distinct and coherent mode of governance, law, and society. It is this form of society that is often taken to characterize a "normal," modern state: the system that historian Paul Johnson calls "the greatest public achievement of the second millennium"; the United Nations and others strive to create in postconflict societies and elsewhere; and conservatives see themselves as defending against the "creeping instrumentalism" of law unmoored from a consensus over the common good.[21]

Two important consequences are often said to follow from this bundle and these give it its normative appeal: it may generate the obligation on individuals to obey the law, thereby producing stability and social quiescence; and it may contribute to valuable, substantive social outcomes, such as respect for individual rights and private property, and lower levels of government corruption.

On the first, the rule of law is sometimes said to be the source of citizens' obligation to follow the law. This obligation can be identified as simultaneously a legal, political, and moral obligation. People are required to obey the law as a matter of law (that is, it is *binding*), politically forced to obey (even accepting that some degree of noncompliance as unavoidable), and morally obligated to the extent that the rule-of-law criteria produce an ethical imperative—if the rules were produced legitimately, it is said, there is a moral obligation on the individual to comply.[22] Taken together, they lead to Raz's conclusion that "people should obey the law and be ruled by it."[23] The rule of law is thus intrinsically linked to the idea of compliance on the part of the subjects, and with a particular theory of social order and modern governance. In a society organized by the rule of law, one is expected to comply with the rules and should be able to trust that others will generally comply with them. This gives order and predictability to society, and marks one kind of transformation from the state of nature to society.

The second effect that follows from the rule-of-law society relates to substantive outcomes: it is frequently claimed that various good things follow from having the legal-political arrangement described above. These include respect for human rights and dignity, a free press, anticorruption, private property and transactions, individual autonomy, the capacity to plan in advance, and more. These outcomes give the rule of law its political appeal, since it is often thought that it represents an institutional arrangement that is more likely to produce them than are other alternative arrangements. This is what Fuller sought to capture with the claim that the rule of law has an "affinity with the good."[24] These valued social goods are understood as *following from* the rule of law, and not as constitutive of its existence. In other words, it sees them as the empirical consequence of the rule of law rather than a component of its definition.

The relation between the rule of law and these substantive goals provides the basis for a key schism in the rule of law literature, between a thick and thin version. In this book, I emphasize the rule of law in "thin," institutional/procedural terms, as a set of rules and practices that organize a society. A competing view takes the position that a rule-of-law system cannot exist unless it is substantively devoted to goals like human rights, equality, or justice. This is a "substantive" or "thick" approach to the rule of law, and requires that the rules enshrine particular social ends, such as equality, liberty, or justice. It arises in the form of a complaint that the thin conception does not clearly rule out social evils (such as

Nazism or torture), if these are permitted or required under the prevailing legal instruments. The thick version makes this conceptually impossible by marrying the idea of the rule of law to a substantive theory of social goods, so that a regime that fails to respect human rights (for instance) can at best be described as performing rule by law, but cannot be characterized as rule of law.[25] In the language of global constitutionalism, this is akin to suggesting that there exists a set of fundamental global norms—perhaps individual rights or the regulation of warfare—that have constitutional status, and against which formal laws can be judged for their constitutionality or lack therefore.[26] This view is common among scholars of world politics and law; it opens the door to the possibility (on the one hand) that states might sometimes rightly break international law to achieve these more important goals and (on the other) that some acts are inherently unlawful if they violate these norms.[27]

Arguing against the thick view, Raz warns that it is a mistake to equate "the rule of law with the rule of the *good* law."[28] He suggests that joining the two together clouds rather than clarifies the relationship among law, politics, and morality. As with all thick theories, it presumes a consensus over goals or morality that the mechanism then is said to enact. It therefore obscures how the mechanism itself (in this case, law) operates.

Despite this and other warnings, though, the tendency to equate the rule of law with substantive social and political goods is common. For instance, the UN secretary-general in 2004 defined the rule of law as "a principle of governance in which all persons . . . are accountable to laws that are [among other things] consistent with international human rights norms and standards."[29] A commitment to human rights norms is thereby defined into the very concept of the rule of law. Similarly, Tom Bingham explains the contribution made by the rule of law by describing society as it would exist in its absence. He says, "The hallmarks of a regime which flouts the rule of law are, alas, all too familiar: the midnight knock on the door, the sudden disappearance, the show trial, the subjection of prisoners to genetic experiment, the confession extracted by torture, the gulag and the concentration camp, the gas chamber, the practice of genocide or ethnic cleansing, the waging of aggressive war. The list is endless."[30] To produce this list, Bingham assumes that the things he finds abhorrent are illegal, with the result that a perfectly faithful adherence to the rule of law will lead to a world in which these things do not happen. He constructs a model of the rule of law in which *noncompliance* with the law is the problem that needs addressing in the pursuit of greater human welfare. Compliance with the law is therefore the path to social good, and noncompliance is the problem to be remedied.[31] This kind of thinking is pervasive in liberal internationalist accounts of the relation between international law and politics, as I examine in later chapters.

I advance a model in this book that sets aside this debate and focuses instead on the practices that are associated with the rule of law in international politics. This requires attention to both the institutions and procedures of law that make legal-political practice possible, and also the substantive ends that people or governments strive to advance by use of these institutions and procedures. This is agnostic about whether important social goods follow from the rule of law, but it insists that they cannot be constitutive of its existence. The thick substantive model assumes too much: it suggests that the question to ask about a legal system is how well it institutionalizes a particular set of goals. Not only does this subordinate the rule of law to a prior theory of what those goals are (which requires that we come to agree on that theory), but it also makes it hard to ask questions about how a legal system is different from other kinds of governance, morality, or politics. A great deal of interesting politics takes place when the demands of the legal system do not map perfectly onto either individual interests or personal morality. The substantive approach presumes that justice and law align neatly with each other. But in the cases that are of interest in this book, there are important phenomena to be studied in the instances and ways that they do not. International treaties are at best imperfect vehicles for justice, and at worst they may actually give governments impunity for the atrocities and other harms they cause. In such cases, even perfect compliance with one's legal obligations does not guarantee that one's actions will be just, for the simple fact that the laws do not neatly reflect the demands of justice.

Can a society embody the three components of the rule of law yet *not* protect (for instance) individual human rights? This is both an empirical and conceptual question. Conceptually, it asks if such a place would deserve to be called a "rule of law society." This is a question about the definition of the rule of law, and many would answer that it cannot. Empirically, it asks whether rule-of-law institutions (properly understood and instituted) necessarily lead to repect for individual human rights. The thin position on the rule of law takes law to exist in the rules and practices of a particular kind of governance along with the structure that upholds them. It presumes that this has interesting political causes and consequences, some of which may be related to achieving justice or other social goods, but not necessarily.

In this section, I have sketched what I take to be a conventional account of the rule of law as it is commonly applied in domestic legal theory. In the next section, I consider the problems that arise when each of these components is brought to bear on the international setting of interstate relations. None can be directly translated to international affairs. The rule of law for world politics therefore must rest on foundations unique to the arrangement of political power and institutions that exist in the international domain. I explore these in the following chapter.

The Domestic Rule of Law in the International System

The three components of the domestic rule of law encounter difficulties when applied to the international setting, each for its own reasons, and this section examines these difficulties. My goal is not to argue against the international rule of law in general. Rather, I show why the international version of the rule of law cannot be simply inferred from the domestic one. I thus argue against the view taken by Judith Goldstein and colleagues in their influential volume on the legalization of world politics; they motivate their project by drawing the domestic rule of law into the international realm, noting that "discourse and institutions normally associated with domestic legal systems have become common in world politics."[32] I show instead that the domestic and international variants are not correspondent concepts; they developed separately, in response to different political needs and challenges, and are based on different arrangements of political power. Their closest connection may come after the fact, in the salutary mode of governance that is alleged to follow from the rule of law in both settings.

PUBLIC, STABLE LAWS?

The first component of the domestic rule of law (that is, that rules be public, stable, and forward-looking) has a simple international analog in the form of the interstate treaty, and more generally, the codification movement from the nineteenth century through to the post–World War II period. The rise of legal positivism in international law, characterized by the belief that state consent is the ultimate source of legal obligation, produced a strong motivation for explicit treaties on a range of subjects, making the treaty the preeminent form of legal instrument. This roughly overlaps with what Martti Koskenniemi has called the "heroic period" for international law from 1870 to 1960.[33]

Treaties are thought to be valuable because they incorporate both the fixity presumed to be required for the rule of law and consent of the subjects (that is, states) through ratification by domestic political institutions. The legal positivist school promotes these two values in the very definition of international law: in the well-known words of the Permanent Court of International Justice in the *Lotus* case, "International law governs relations between independent States. The rules of law binding upon States therefore emanate from their own free will."[34] Consent to a formal text is, for Theresa Reinold and Michael Zürn, the most direct means by which international law can achieve its "core objective," which they summarize as to "stabilize actors' normative expectations in an otherwise volatile world and shield them from . . . the vicissitudes of politics." To do so, it is required "that legal rules display certain features, such as transparency, clarity, non-retroactivity, etc."[35] Treaties are widely thought to embody these characteristics and therefore the codification of international law is often equated with its "progressive development."[36]

The codification of international law was a notable project in twentieth-century global politics. From the opening decades of the twentieth century, it is evident at the heart of the Covenant of the League of Nations (which demanded "a scrupulous respect for all treaty obligations") as well as in Woodrow Wilson's Fourteen Points (whose first principle is "open covenants, openly arrived at"), and in the league's Committee of Experts for the Progressive Codification of International Law and its 1930 Conference on Codification. Midcentury, the United Nations was founded on a commitment to "the progressive development of international law and its codification" through the General Assembly (UN Charter, Art. 13). This mandate produced the International Law Commission, which took over from the League's Committee of Experts in 1947, as a permanent body of international-legal professionals dedicated to expanding the scope of international law by codifying it. In the words of the International Law Commission's constitution, its goal is to advance "the more precise formulation and systematization of rules of international law" and prepare "draft conventions on subjects which have not yet been regulated by international law."[37] The codification movement sees it as a success that the number of interstate treaties has grown exponentially. As the UN secretary-general said recently, "Treaties are a critical foundation to the rule of law."[38]

The drive for codified law can be understood as the operationalization of the first piece of the rule-of-law ideology: the requirement for clear and stable rules. Explicit, well-written law is believed to make a particularly powerful contribution to international order. This is reflected in the modern "legalization" project among scholars of law and political science. Goldstein and colleagues suggest that "fully legalized institutions bind states through law: their behavior is subject to scrutiny under general rules, procedures, and discourse of international law and, often, domestic law. Legalized institutions also demonstrate a high degree of precision, meaning that their rules unambiguously define the conduct they require, authorize, or proscribe."[39] The stability and clarity of the rules are essential in the "move to law" that these authors identify. These are the qualities that Thomas Franck identified as constituting the "determinacy" of a rule: "that which makes its message clear." And while "some degree of indeterminacy is inevitable in any body of rules . . . indeterminacy also has its costs, which are paid in the coin of legitimacy."[40] "Indeterminate normative standards make it harder to know what is expected."[41] "The more determinate a standard, the most difficult it is to justify noncompliance."[42] Legalization changes the calculations of actors because it specifies whether an action is permitted or not. It gives others a standard by which to judge the state as compliant or not, and supplies a basis for states' reputations regarding rule following and rule breaking. Clarity and stability are the essence of international law.

Neither in theory nor practice does international law offer this stability and clarity.

Against all this scholarship is the fact that individual states have the capacity to change the legal status of their behavior—from illegal to legal, from violation to compliance—by the exercise of their legal and political agency. This is unthinkable in the classic domestic rule of law where the legality of an act is set by the state, not the actor. At the international level, states themselves choose which obligations will apply to them, and they do so as individuals.

This does not negate the international rule of law; instead it signals that the relationship between codification and the rule of law is different in the international context than it is in the domestic one. A clear rule does not mean a clear obligation, and the presence of an obligation does not mean there is consensus over the meaning of compliance.

Codified rules of international law wait on state consent, and consent is a product of state agency. The existence of a treaty cannot in itself be read to imply an obligation on the part of a state. As a consequence, one cannot ask what international law is on a given topic (say, hunting whales on the high seas) and expect an answer that is generalizable across states. Instead, one must ask what the law is *for a given state*, and perhaps even *in relation to a specific other state*, and then find the answer in the treaties, protocols, and rules of custom that apply to that state. For whale hunting, the legal obligations taken on by Australia under the International Whaling Convention are different than those taken on by Iceland (which has formally objected to certain provisions of the treaty), and both are different than those that apply to Turkey (which has not signed the convention). The same act—for instance, taking a whale on the high seas in the Southern Ocean—has a different legal status depending on which of these states committed it. It is a violation of international law for Australia to permit an Australian vessel to hunt whales. It is not a violation for Iceland to allow Icelandic ships to do the same.[43] Turkey, because it has not signed the treaty, has an unlimited right to hunt whales.[44]

States retain the right and capacity to withdraw or modify their consent, and thus their obligations, when it serves their needs. Behavior that was a legal violation when North Korea was a member of the Treaty on the Non-Proliferation of Nuclear Weapons may no longer be a violation after it removed itself from the treaty.[45] An International Criminal Court state that fails to extradite a suspect to that body may be noncompliant with its treaty obligations, but the noncompliance may disappear if the state enters into an Article 98 agreement relevant to that suspect that requires it to refrain from extraditing them. The legal and political arguments that arise around these cases (for instance, on interpreting Article 98 agreements in the Rome Statute, or how North Korea's Non-Proliferation Treaty obligations relate to subsequent UN Security Council decisions) illustrate the broader point that the meaning of compliance and noncompliance depend on the details of states' particular commitments. Stable, public, and uniform legal obligations are not characteristic of the international rule of law.

Much of international law is devoted to managing the degrees of freedom enjoyed by states as they exercise their agency over their legal obligations. This includes the Vienna Convention on the Law of Treaties along with its rules on the denunciation of and withdrawing from treaties, adding or changing reservations, fundamental changes in circumstances, obligations and government succession, the relation of subsequent treaties to prior treaties on the same subject, and so on.[46] These rules limit how states might use the autonomy that they possess to redefine their legal obligations—but they do not eliminate that autonomy, and as Larry Helfer has noted, states remain in a position to redefine the legality of their actions.[47]

The goal of a unified set of public rules that apply to all subjects cannot be achieved or even approximated in the interstate setting because states retain the individual capacity to accept, reject, or modify their legal obligations through treaty accession, reservations, and persistent objections. Each state could potentially have a unique set of legal obligations. There can be no general answer to the legality of many international acts: from torture to nuclear research to labor standards to whale hunting, for each state one must ask what rules it has accepted, and what reservations or understandings it has imposed on those acceptances. This is equally true of customary international law as it is of treaties. Customary law does not bind states if they make persistent objections to its application to them as the rule is coming into being.[48] Each government constructs its own set of legal obligations and fine-tunes it through reservations. Domestic legal subjects cannot do this.

Norms of *jus cogens* may stand as an exception to this generalization. These are rules from which, by definition, no derogation is allowed, and as such they are presumed to apply, and apply equally, to all states. The content of this set is open for debate, but its existence is well accepted. It is provided for in the Vienna Convention on the Law of Treaties in Article 53, which says that "a treaty is void, if, at the time of its conclusion, it conflicts with a peremptory [*jus cogens*] norm of general international law." The most compelling candidates for such norms are the rules against genocide, aggression, the acquisition of territory by force, and piracy, and for the self-determination of peoples.[49] The rules against genocide were noted by the ICJ in the *Democratic Republic of Congo v. Rwanda* case, and for self-determination in the *East Timor* case in 1995.[50] In relation to the ban on torture, *jus cogens* is discussed in the various opinions of the *Belgium v. Senegal* ICJ decision of 2012 and *Furundzija* case at the International Criminal Tribunal for the Former Yugoslavia.[51] To the extent that such rules exist, they make the international legal domain more comparable to the domestic domain in that they are unquestionably in a position of superior authority over individual subjects. The substantive scope of this category is narrow, however, and within those bounds individual rules are highly contested. *Jus cogens* therefore helps to show what the main body of international law is *not*: a set of shared, public, stable rules that apply equally to all subjects.

In sum, the international legal system cannot satisfy the standard expectation in a rule-of-law society that law be clear, stable, and known in advance. No matter how clearly it is written, international law will not indicate definitively that an action is legal or illegal. We need more information about what the state in question has said or done. Because states are free to tailor their commitments to suit their needs and interests through the careful use of consent, reservations, treaty exit, public statements, and more, the bundle of laws that attach to each state are unique to that state, and the legality of an act may not be determinable in advance. What it means to comply with a rule depends on who is doing it, what that state has done and said about it in the past, and what it might do and say in the present case. The same act may be legal when committed by one state but illegal when committed by another; it may be legal when committed toward one state but illegal toward another. The legality of an act is endogenous to the choices of the state in question rather than independent of it as it is in the domestic setting.

GOVERNMENT LIMITED BY LAW?

The second component of the domestic rule of law is the requirement that law apply to the government as well as to the citizens. This is a solution to the problem of despotic leaders. It implies that the legal system should be an instrument for limiting the government's authority over citizens and perhaps subjecting it to the will of the people, somehow defined. It can be seen as preserving the autonomy of the legal sphere from the political, ensuring that law is superordinate over government, or protecting individuals' liberty from the state.[52]

The international analog to this is difficult to find: if the international rule of law is understood with reference to how the government is made accountable under law, then what is the international "government"?

The simplest answer is to say that there is none, on the theory that the interstate political space is missing the central political institution and therefore is an anarchy in a specific sense.[53] This accords the standard model of "international anarchy" that is represented in international relations theory in various forms by Kenneth Waltz, Hedley Bull, Alexander Wendt, and others. This is the "anarchy problematique."[54] It is the premise of much international theory scholarship, and suggests that the fundamental difference between domestic and international society is the presence of government in the former yet its absence in the latter.

This framing of the problem of international law may be sustainable if one takes the narrowest view of what constitutes "government"—a centralized, authoritative, coercive institution kept in power by the twin forces of legitimacy and coercion. The institution of state sovereignty presumes that world government does not exist, and hence the distinctive features of international law are often seen as a result of the attempts by states to manage their relations of interdependence in its absence.[55] This is the thought behind Immanuel Kant's "Second Definitive Article for a Perpetual Peace": "As nations, peoples can be regarded as single individuals who injure one another through their close proximity while living in the state of nature. . . . For the sake of its own security, each nation can and should demand that the others enter into a contract resembling the civil one and guaranteeing the rights of each."[56]

Most scholars, however, no longer subscribe to this absolutist view of international anarchy. Across the range of IR theory perspectives, it is widely accepted that various forms and degrees of governance exist in the interstate system, and as a consequence, scholarship has turned to examine the extent to which agents other than a centralized formal institution perform the functions of governance in international society. These might include quasi-public regulation by private actors, contracts or coordination among legal equals, Great Power leadership or dominion, pooled sovereignty organizations, transnational class factions, and other legitimated international institutions.[57] While none meet a formalist's definition of government, they all provide evidence of disaggregated governance among states and sometimes exercise great influence over the processes of international (and perhaps domestic) life. Harold Koh suggests that we should think of state sovereignty in terms of the functions performed by a sovereign (rather than the centralized bureaucracy that frequently houses those functions), which may mean that these diverse institutions of international governance can be said to exercise sovereignty.[58] These practices contradict the claim that the international system is an anarchy in the sense defined by Waltz, Bull, and others.[59]

It follows, then, that "governance without government" may exist at the international level, and so the international rule of law may be expected to regulate its institutions.[60] Two possibilities are worth considering as locations for international government that might be regulated by the international rule of law: strong states or the UN system.

First, following Gerry Simpson and others, we might see the international legal system as entrusting the most powerful states with the functions of governance over the rest of the international system, and in this case, we should ask whether the international rule of law requires that these agents be limited by international law. It is often said that certain states (or the Great Powers as a class) have special responsibilities toward the international system, composed of rights and obligations for the maintenance of international order that do not attach to rank-and-file states. Claims about the importance of Great Power leadership, hegemonic stability, and collective security all rest on this premise.[61] In this view, Tamanaha's category of government limited by law might be satisfied in the international system by ensuring that the strongest states be bound by international law. This they certainly are in a formal sense, but it is clear also that they have greater capacity to bear the costs of lawbreaking and greater influence in rule making, both by dominating diplomacy where rules are negotiated and by the rules of recognition for customary law—in short, the practices of certain states matter more in identifying customary international law.

The tendency for international law to change its meaning under the influence of strong states means that it is unlikely that the international rule of law can rest on the degree to which the law as it is written binds the international community or some "leading" states. On the contrary, it is common to see customary law as changing due to changes in state practice, especially by the leading states. This is precisely the conventional theory of how customary law develops, but it is also evident in relation to treaties. The UN Security Council practice of treating abstentions by permanent members as something other than a veto arose in this way. This has been the consistent practice since the earliest days of the Council and yet it contradicts the plain meaning of the Charter clause that regulates voting in the Council. The first time the practice was used (in 1946) the irate ambassador from the Soviet Union stormed from the room in protest, but its repeated use and practical advantages quickly extinguished any controversy.[62] Today, it is widely accepted as an informal revision of the Charter, and was affirmed by the ICJ in a 1971 opinion that rejected South Africa's claim that a resolution against it was illegal because three permanent members had abstained when it was passed.[63]

A similar development has underwritten the concept of humanitarian intervention since 1990. The use of force by states is illegal under the UN Charter unless authorized by the Security Council, and no distinction is made in the Charter for war motivated by humanitarian rescue. The development of responsibility to protect and other doctrines has arguably legalized humanitarian intervention even without Council approval.[64] The case in favor of the legality of humanitarian intervention rests on recent developments in practice among states, international organizations, and others in favor of the practice. Together, these form the foundation of the assertion that a progressive development in the law has taken place so that Council approval is not necessarily a requirement for legal intervention.

In relation to both Security Council abstention and humanitarian intervention, powerful players in world politics decided that the new interpretation was a desirable improvement over the plain language of existing treaties and thus the new practice should not be considered rule breaking. This represents the collective legitimation of violation, "constructive noncompliance," by which apparent violations are transformed into revisions of the law.[65]

One might alternately identify international government with the United Nations or another formal international organization. It would then be normal to ask how international law limits that body. This may amount to seeing the UN Charter as the constitution of the international system, but it need not go that far.[66] The argument is particularly relevant for the UN Security Council with its decisive governing authority over the member states of the United Nations under the Charter. Its powers include the right to decide when to use force against member states, the right to act on behalf of all states when taking a decision, and the right to decide on its own sphere on competence. Together, these look very much like the Weberian definition of a state—a centralized agent that holds a monopoly on the legitimate use of force—and the Security Council may be a kind of world government.[67] Moreover, the Council undoubtedly has the authority to make law that is binding on all states, both in relation to specific threats to international peace and security, and more generally in its recent "legislative" mode, insisting on certain policies of all states.[68] If the Security Council (or the United Nations) is a form of international government, then it might follow that the Council or the United Nations must be situated within a setting of legal rules that limit its autonomy relative to its subjects (presumably, states).

The Council's relationship to international law has long been debated, beginning with the organization's prehistory in San Francisco in 1945 when the United States and others defeated a proposal to explicitly make the Council subordinate to international law all the way to *Kadi* in the Court of Justice of the European Union recently.[69] The UN Charter stakes a clear position on this matter, affirming that the Council is a political rather than a legal organ, and that it responds to "threats to international peace and security" instead of violations of international law. Subsequent practice has upheld the view that the Council does not decide legal issues.[70] For instance, Article 24(1) describes the Council as having "primary responsibility for the maintenance of international peace and security" with no mention of international law, in contrast to the ICJ, which is described as the "principal judicial organ of the United Nations" (Art. 92).[71] When the Council does create legal obligations on UN members by using its powers in Chapter VII, these must be understood as legal demands regarding political policy choices, not settlements of legal disputes themselves.

Whether the Council itself is required to follow international law is an open question. It is clear that it must abide by the Charter, but it is arguable whether the Council is superior or subordinate to the rest of international law. The rationale for its superiority comes from the fact that the Charter authorizes the Council to impose any solution it desires in response to a threat to international peace and security. It follows that it is not limited by international law in doing so. On this reading, the Council could not (for instance) undertake an enforcement action for any purpose other than "to maintain or restore international peace and security" (Art. 39), but it could demand that states seize the assets of foreign governments or foreign nationals in a manner that would normally violate international laws on expropriation. This points to an "imperial Council," in which the Charter authorizes the Council to stand above international law.[72] The contrary assertion, for its subordination to international law, rests on the view that since it is *constituted* by international law through the treaty process, it is therefore in no position to act outside it. The *Kadi II* decision of the Court of Justice of the European Union asked but did not answer the key question of whether that court could invalidate a duly passed resolution of the Council that conflicts with European law.

A second-order question concerns whether there exists an international institution with the competence to review the legality of Council actions. The ICJ is the most logical candidate for such a role, though this is in considerable doubt; the ICJ has had several opportunities to exercise judicial review of the Council and it has avoided explicitly claiming that right.[73] Alvarez notes that "the World Court [ICJ] has never found any action taken by any UN organ to be illegal in a binding context," and suggests that doing so "would provoke a political crisis and appears unlikely given the limits on the ICJ's jurisdiction, as well as gaps in international law."[74] In both the *Namibia* and *Lockerbie* cases, the Court was asked questions that implicated the limits of Council authority, but in both it declined to provide a decisive interpretation either way.[75] Judge Stephen Schwebel said in the *Lockerbie* case (as summarized by the ICJ),

That raises the question of whether the Court possesses a power of judicial review over Council decisions. In Judge Schwebel's view, the Court is not generally so empowered. . . .

The Court has more than once disclaimed a power of judicial review. The terms of the Charter furnish no shred of support for such power. In fact, they import the contrary, since, if the Court could overrule the Council, it would be it and not the Council which would exercise dispositive and hence primary authority in a sphere in which the Charter accords primary authority to the Council.[76]

This does not lead to the conclusion that international organizations are in general not bound by international law. They clearly are, with a small number of possible exceptions—notably, the UN Security Council when acting under Chapter VII of the Charter and the ICJ when deciding a case *ex aequo et bono* under Article 38(2) of the ICJ Statute. Instead, it shows that the domestic ideal of a government subordinated under law does not apply unproblematically to the international context since it presumes answers to a host of deep (and perhaps-unanswerable) questions about the nature and location of government or governance at the international level.

RULES APPLIED CONSISTENTLY ACROSS CASES?

The third element commonly cited in the domestic rule of law is that rules should be applied dispassionately and similarly across similar cases. This suggests that the content of the law should be constant and be applied constantly, regardless of the identity of the actor. As with the other two elements, this idea meets decisive obstacles in the international realm in that international legal obligations are founded on precisely the opposite principle: that the identity of the state is an essential consideration in assessing the international lawfulness of an act.

At one level, the idea of legal equality is central to the self-understanding of international law in the sense that each sovereign state is said to begin as a legal person with equal rights and obligations to all other states. Article 2(1) of the UN Charter codifies this into what amounts to a legal premise for the interstate system: "The Organization is based on the principle of the sovereign equality of all its Members." Equality is enshrined in many other instruments and practices, including the ICJ Statute (Art. 35), nondiscrimination rules in the World Trade Organization, the law of treaties as embodied in the Vienna Convention on the Law of Treaties, and much more. The legal personality that underlies the existence of a sovereign state is usually understood to be a bundle of rights and obligations that is precisely the same for all states. With all this weight placed behind sovereign equality, deviations from equality carry the burden of explanation—they stand in need of justification, defense, or explanation.

In practice, however, this expression of sovereign equality moves the international legal-political system *away from* rather than toward the idea of legal equality as imagined in the domestic rule of law. As authors of their own legal obligations, for states the equal application of the law means something different than it does among individuals. First, states' legal rights and obligations diverge as soon as some of them consent to treaties. Each acquires a distinctive portfolio of obligations, with the effect noted above that the lawfulness of a particular act is thus depends on which state is doing it. Second, the absence of compulsory jurisdiction means that court decisions are equally particularistic, since states possess the negative right to *not* be bound by the legal decisions of others. This is explicit in the ICJ Statute, which says ICJ decisions "have no binding force except between the parties and in respect of that particular case" (Art. 59). Third, it is obvious that states have unequal influence on making and remaking international rules; the statements, acts, and interests of some count for more in international legalization, sometimes formally and sometimes informally.[77] This is equally true of customary international law as it is of treaties.[78] And while this is sometimes dismissed as merely a deviation from the ideal of equality, it is in fact well integrated into the practices and institutions of legalization and legal interpretation; it has been "normalized," as Simpson and others have shown.

In sum, the international legal system demands in various ways that the legal affairs of states be understood in particularist terms—as the expression of the specific circumstances of the parties involved. It cannot treat legal obligations as consistent across the identities of various states. In many areas of international law, there can be no general answer to the legality of an act: to determine what actions are lawful for a state, one must first know what rules it has accepted, and what reservations or understandings it has imposed on those acceptances.

States possess more freedom toward particular rules of international law than is compatible with the rule of law as understood in domestic affairs. They have the legal right to accept or reject them, and some practical capacity to redefine them, as they wish. This is especially striking for strong states, as these are given greater weight in the ongoing interpretation of rules in practice and have greater capacity to write, resist, and enforce rules as they wish.

Each of the three pillars often thought to be essential to the domestic rule of law is contradicted by fundamental elements of the interstate system. Sovereign states do not accept that they are automatically bound by stable, shared rules applied equally and dispassionately across cases horizontally, and vertically between agents and a "government." As a consequence, it is clear that the international rule of law cannot be deduced from the domestic version.

Conclusion

The universalism of the rule of law ideology contrasts with the particularism of states' specific legal obligations. The tension between fragmentation and unity, which is often seen as bedeviling the development of a coherent international legal system, in fact shows a way forward for thinking about the international rule of law.[79] It neatly separates that which is universal and uncontested from that which is particular and contested. In the conventional account of international law, the former consists of the general expectation that states will act in accordance with international law (that is, the international rule of law) and the latter contains the actual substantive obligations that apply to them. The latter varies from state to state and is subject to active reconstruction by states through the mechanisms discussed above.[80] The former is essentially unquestioned in world politics today and it is what I identify as the international rule of law. This commitment might be conceived as occupying a constitutional position in the international political system. This insight helps show the hidden politics of the international rule of law—a set of liberal political commitments that depoliticize power relations and are embedded in the conventional "legalization" project in IR.[81]

The international rule of law refers to the intellectual and political commitment—Shirley Scott's "ideology"—to the idea that all state behavior should conform to whatever international legal obligations relate to it and that the result of executing this commitment faithfully is a well-ordered international space.[82] It exists in the widespread belief that states should conduct themselves according to international law, which in practice means that they will use the resources of international law to explain and justify their policies. This is the constitutional meta-norm that makes international diplomacy and politics recognizably contemporary: giving, receiving, and arguing over the legal reasoning that authorizes state acts.[83]

The use of international law as a legitimating discourse is pervasive in contemporary international politics. States almost without fail provide public explanations for how their behavior is consistent with their legal obligations and routinely use the charge of "illegality" to delegitimate the acts of others that they oppose. This practice, and the expectation that others will engage in it, provides the structure for world politics. Law is the language that states use to understand and explain their acts, goals, and desires, and is both internal and external to state interests.

With this role in international affairs, the international rule of law comes to be "constitutional" in world politics in the sense of providing the fundamental rules within which the normal conduct of politics and contestation takes place.[84] It is a structure of authority that is in a position of hierarchy over actors, and makes possible the "ordinary political contestation and disagreement" that make up everyday international politics.[85]

Taking this approach changes how the relations between international law and international politics can be studied. It abandons the liberal presumption that the rule of law is a neutral, nonpolitical framework for politics and opens up new lines of inquiry. It requires an explicitly instrumental approach to international law.[86] It is normal for all parties to claim to represent the fact of compliance, and they construct arguments in defense of that position using the legal resources of the past, adapted to present needs. Legal resources and categories are used by states to frame their choices, and specifically to legitimate them by showing them to be lawful. These legal justifications are not deliberative procedures in the sense envisioned by theorists of communicative action—they are not based on public reasons or reasoning, and there is no expectation that they will lead to a *telos* of consensus. They are instead self-interested and instrumental, but based on communal resources of international law with its internal logic and particular structure.[87] States are continually engaged in showing that they are complying with their obligations. They interpret the rules and their own behavior in such a way that the two coincide. This often means stretching the rules in ways that may be controversial, and also implies the inability to take actions for which no resources of justification exist.[88] In other words, law is both constraining and empowering. These are the subjects of the next chapter.

3

How to Do Things with International Law

The concepts and structures of international law . . . are the conditions of possibility for the existence of something like a sphere of the international.
—MARTTI KOSKENNIEMI, *FROM APOLOGY TO UTOPIA*

The idea that international law is or can be "a set of rules . . . applied even-handedly between weak and strong . . . on all occasions" is appealing but it omits much of the politics central to international law.[1] This classical liberal view, discussed in the previous chapter, is blind to the role of power in the international legal system as it actually exists. I ask instead that we follow where the evidence leads and take seriously the use of international law as a strategic tool. An account along these lines would be more realistic; it would affirm that in practice, law and politics are closely intertwined, even inseparable.

This account must differ from the classical view in three key ways. It must recognize law's *instrumental utility* to governments, its *productive power* in foreign policy discourse and international affairs, and its coconstitution with *power politics*. Such a model is hardly outlandish. Since the early twentieth century, and more recently in the international arena, legal realists have emphasized law in practice.[2] Observers of global affairs have long acknowledged that governments use international law for legitimation and justification and that international law encodes substantive political commitments.[3] The use of practice as a unit of analysis involving both agent and structure is common in social theory and gaining popularity in IR.[4]

I bring these strands together into an account of the international rule of law that highlights its political power. It subordinates governments underneath the authority of law and legalism and thus empowers governments to take up legal arguments to legitimize their choices. This analytic starting point brings into focus the interrelation between law and legalism on the one hand and global power politics on the other. This chapter sets out this framework and the following chapters use it to trace the political utility of law in contemporary world politics.

Instrumentalism and the International Rule of Law

International law is political because it is useful. Governments and others invoke it to present their policies, goals, and complaints and argue over which actions are legal. And international law is useful because of the widespread belief in rule-of-law ideology, whereby acting lawfully is a determinant of state legitimacy.

If states operate within a political structure that rewards compliance with international law, then they also have incentive to frame their choices and goals within legal categories. Doing so is important because it enables them to maintain good standing while achieving strategic ends. That is why I describe international law as a resource with productive power. This resource is available to nonstate actors as well. Jessica Stanton has shown that rebel groups sometimes change strategy in order to align with international humanitarian law—the better to win support for their struggles. Similarly, NGOs often advance their goals through legal cases as well as rhetoric and activism mobilizing international law.[5]

Asserting compliance with international law is an integral part of today's public diplomacy.[6] Governments profess to engage in peacekeeping rather than colonial occupation, enhanced interrogation rather than torture, self-defense rather than aggression; use space resources rather than claim sovereignty over celestial bodies; protect religious freedom rather than impose standards of belief and practice; and perform scientific research rather than commercial whaling.[7] One could cite many more examples.

These are not mere euphemisms; they are artifacts of international law. The distinctions within a given dyad are significant and depend on the terms of treaties and other legal sources. Disputes occur in formal legal settings, as when the Philippines argued that China's activities in the South China Sea violated its legal rights. And they occur in foreign policy discourse generally, as in 2013, when the United States condemned the Syrian government's deployment of chemical weapons as "a crime against humanity, and a violation of the laws of war."[8]

An instrumental view of the power of law is out of favor in many discussions of international law and politics. Indeed, it is often presented as *mis*use of the law, more associated with lawfare and the rule by law than the rule of law itself.[9] The appropriate response to legal rules, it is said, is compliance not strategic behavior. Thus Samantha Besson, a follower of Raz and H.L.A. Hart, argues the power of international law can be seen as "content-independent."[10] She suggests that its influence is revealed by states' compliance, no matter the impact on their particular interests. In other words, law works when agents defer to it based on their obligations alone.

This effort to isolate international law and legalization from the substantive interests and goals of actors has always been a mistake, as both research method and substantive assumption about how international politics work. Yet it was ascendent, for a time. In the 1990s, IR conventional wisdom held that state behavior originates *either* from an instrumental attitude toward outcomes *or* from a normative feeling of obligation to the rules.[11] James March and Johan Olsen did much to legitimate this apparent distinction.

Their logics of consequences and appropriateness helped to institutionalize a disciplinary divide between people who studied material payoffs, strategic thinking, and interests, and those who studied norms, socialization, ideas, and beliefs about appropriate behavior.[12] But the wall was bound to crumble because neither side could say much about the world without the other. And so, despite some remnants, the field of IR has largely moved on to the social construction of strategic behavior, bringing together practices, power, institutions, and interests.

I take this more encompassing approach. On this view, instrumentalism is not a failure of law, sign of weakness, or problem to be fixed. It is instead a feature of the international legal system operating according to its internal logic—the logic of rule following and legitimation through legality. I see this as an explanation of the idea of law and not a critique. There would be no law-based justifications if actors were not generally committed to the importance of compliance and the rule of law. These are taken for granted within the international social environment, which is why it is essential that scholars pay attention to legalization's effects.

The utility of law should be our starting point because it hints that international law and state interests are closely related. Accepting the reality of instrumentalism leads to a series of research questions about the constitution of legal resources, background conditions that make this possible, and constraining and empowering effects of operating in a legalized environment.

This does not mean that law can be ignored in favor of interests alone, nor does it mean that governments can do whatever they want regardless of law. Instead, it means we should consider how state interests and the content of international law are mutually reinforcing. Each, at least in part, constitutes the other. Governments' aims, and their capacity to achieve them, are to some degree determined by the categories and powers of international law, and vice versa. That governments use legal concepts to their own ends does not mean law is unimportant. Precisely the opposite. State practice invests in law's discursive authority.

Productive Power and the International Rule of Law

Oscar Schachter, the mid-twentieth-century international lawyer and diplomat, was on to something when he wrote, "A skilled and perceptive 'peace-keeper' will find that persuasion is immensely facilitated by invoking legal obligations and prescriptions."[13] This special persuasive capacity of law is founded in presumptions about rule following: because governments are expected to fulfill their international legal obligations, claims about compliance and noncompliance are consequential. The productive power of international law is therefore a product of political commitment to the rule of law.

Where rule following is an important sign of legitimacy, legalization has opportunities to flourish. In essence, legalization is a process in which words and concepts are invested with the capacity to distinguish lawful from unlawful behavior.[14] The morality and strategic wisdom of a given policy become secondary to questions of law and legality, the answers to which depend on how states interpret their obligations. This is the mechanism by which legalization provides resources for justifying and criticizing policy choices. What actors do with these resources depends on their political interests. Thus, eschewing moral and strategic concerns, lawyers can argue about whether waterboarding is or is not torture *as a legal matter*. The same is true of competing claims about aggression, religious freedom, science, and so on. Once these are defined as legal categories, states and other actors seek the benefits of legitimation by supplying legal justifications. Or conversely, actors can use legal categories to make the case that an adversary is behaving unlawfully, even if its actions are prudent and humanitarian.

The use of force in self-defense provides a good example. In chapter 4 I show that the UN Charter facilitates the use of force by providing self-defense as an iron-clad legal justification. Regardless of the outcome or true motives of military action, the justification of self-defense, when backed by law, fosters legitimacy. It is important to keep in mind, though, that the value of these legal narratives is not inherent to them but rather socially constructed in the course of interactions among global actors. Self-defense, humanitarian intervention, nonintervention, and respect for borders are "symbolic tokens" of modernity, as described by Anthony Giddens and Zygmunt Bauman: they are resources agents deploy to signal membership in virtuous groups or adherence to virtuous ways of thinking.[15] Virtue has been presumed inherent in all these activities—humanitarian intervention, preventing atrocities; nonintervention, manifesting self-restraint; respect for borders, creating a stable world order.

Today, it is rule following that signals good international citizenship, even if the rules are sometimes so malleable that their outputs are ambiguous. Reputation may hinge less on successfully proving that one's actions are lawful and more on making a legible claim of legality using the standard repertoire of legal arguments and resources. This acknowledges that black-letter law will always contain ambiguity and that it requires some interpretation in order to make it fit the real world. Interpretation is not blind to the political consequences that follow from it—that is, states and legal observers know which interpretations will legitimize their preferred outcomes and which will not.

As governments use international law in their foreign policies, they seek the maximum advantage from these ambiguities. There is nothing surprising about this. However, it fuels a recursive dynamic between legal obligations and state interests as the self-serving legal interpretations of governments motivated to accomplish some short-term goal become resources that are used to inform future readings of the law. This can reliably be expected to move the law toward interpretations favored by the strongest states, as it is their practice that is most persuasive in resolving conflicts over the meaning of the rules.

Legal categories also show their muscle by defining the content and limits of rights, responsibilities, obligations, and liabilities.[17] A classic example is the determination of responsibility for killing in war: where the legal condition of war obtains between two parties, soldiers on one side who kill soldiers of the other side cannot be said to have committed murder.[18] Similarly, states' liability for accidental deaths is reduced in wartime, as compared with peacetime. As I discuss in more detail in chapter 6, US drone strikes are arguably lawful if the United States is in a state of war with the targets and unlawful if it is not.

Social theorists such as Pierre Bourdieu, Charles Taylor, Giddens, and Theodore Schatzki have mapped such processes of justification in various ways.[19] The dialogic quality of legal justification makes it a paradigm case of a social practice. It relies on, makes use of, and invests in shared understandings about the relationship between law and politics. Jutta Brunnée and Stephen Toope argue that international law is a "community of practice" in which "shared understandings become background knowledge or norms that shape how actors perceive themselves and the world, how they form interests and set priorities, and how they make or evaluate arguments."[20] This social ontology yields research methods in which agents and structures exist in a recursive, mutually implicating relationship.[21]

This is the bread and butter of practice theory: "practices . . . mediate the relation between agents and social structures, constituting both agential identities and interests and intersubjective systems of meaning."[22] Charlotte Peevers observes, "When states justify their interventions they draw on and articulate shared values and expectations that other decision-makers and publics in other states hold. . . . [J]ustification is literally an attempt to connect one's actions with standards of justice or, more generically, with standards of appropriate and acceptable behavior."[23] Peevers, Janina Dill, Emmanuel Adler, Vincent Pouliot, Friedrich Kratochwil, and others have considered the implications of social practice for IR and international law.[24]

As governments use these intersubjective meanings to understand and communicate their actions, they engage in what the organizational sociologist Karl Weick calls "sensemaking": the process by which "agents construct sensible, sensable events" out of their experiences in the world.[25] This sensemaking situates the actor and its choices within a context of meaning already existing in the society. Sensemaking cannot be the act of a radically autonomous, individuated agent.[26]

In the legal context, sensemaking draws from a specifically *legal* set of resources and logics rather than from other possible sources. As Frank Michelman explains, "To furnish a *legal* justification for a decision is to show that the decision is according to law."[27] Treaties and legal texts, along with past state practice and other sources, are put to use in a specifically legal form of argumentation in order to construct or justify action. At least in theory, nonlegal sources are ignored; Neil MacCormack describes a "special sort of [juridical] reasoning . . . which leaves aside any general and abstract deliberation on what in a given context it would be best or would be all things considered right to do or not go. Where law is appealed to, not all things are considered."[28] As Veitch notes, "One key feature of the distinctiveness of these [legal] categories [is that] . . . there is an ability—in fact, a *duty*—to refer to sources of legal authority as embodied in a range of legal texts, including constitutions, custom, statutes, case reports, etc."[29]

International legal explanation is a form of sensemaking in that it involves actors drawing on the sorts of resources Veitch lists, interpreting them as they relate to the current situation and presenting them as reasons for action. In practice, they are the means by which a state suggests, for example, that its use of force is an instance of humanitarianism rather than imperialism; it is expropriating foreign assets for security reasons, not to enrich itself; aerial drone attack is an acceptable tactic in a lawful war against a nonstate enemy rather than an assault on the sovereignty or territory of another country. Among the resources consulted in this sensemaking process, international law ranks highly.

This was not always the case. Before law and legality supplied a legitimating discourse in global affairs—and alongside them, to some extent—states turned to other sources of justification, such as divine right, economic exigency, self-preservation, ethnic self-determination, claims to modernity, and scientific racism. I do not examine how law came to be such a vital resource among others, studies of which can be found elsewhere. Ikenberry, Ruti Teitel, and Mary Ellen O'Connell, for instance, chart the behavioral manifestations of legalization, including the growth in formal international organizations with explicit legal personalities or mandates to adjudicate disputes through law.[30] Koskenniemi, Reus-Smit, Brunnée and Toope, Mark Mazower, and Benjamin Coates discuss the intellectual foundations on which these institutions rest—specifically, the historical developments that installed a generalized belief in legal institutions as the natural, appropriate, or expeditious means to carry out international affairs.[31] Relatedly, Jennifer Mitzen describes the emergence of a shared intellectual framework that organized nineteenth-century European state justifications.[32] I will let these scholars speak for themselves, as my interest is in the uses and effects of the international rule of law, not in the origins of legal obligation.[33]

Conclusion: Power Politics and the International Rule of Law

Given the uses states make of international law, the standard formulation of law as a constraint on autonomy needs to be reconsidered.

This convention is baked into the terms of IR. Law is widely understood to be not only distinct from power but also antithetical to it. As Georg Sørensen puts it, "A purely power-based order is thin and shaky because it lacks legitimacy, the lawfulness that follows from being authorized by institutional consent."[34] For Simmons, constraint is inherent in international law, "an explicit, public, and lawlike promise by public authorities to act within particular boundaries in their relationships."[35] Arthur Watts says that international law "tells [governments] there are certain things they cannot do."[36] This way of thinking crosses liberal and realist boundaries: both camps measure the effectiveness of law by its ability to prevent governments, especially strong ones, from doing what they want.[37]

The liberal-realist divide in IR theory is essentially about whether the answer is yes or no—can international law really constrain states? Realists argue in the negative: strong states, they note, can mostly choose when to comply with international law, shape the rules according to their interests, and force weaker states to abide by rules they themselves evade.[38] In response, IR liberals show that even strong states are sometimes persuaded, compelled, or naturally inclined to comply with international law. If power does at times concede to law, then realists must be wrong.[39] Liberals are described as "optimists" with respect to the constraining power of international law, and realists "pessimists."[40] Yet both sides believe that law, when it works, negates power. They also share a normative commitment to constraint.

But I show that the rule of law is in fact a product of social practice, in which legal explanation furnishes political justification. It is empowering as well as constraining. Whether a state is bound by a given law is often a matter of its own choosing, and when it is so bound, it has wide latitude to interpret the law in ways that advance its own goals. It is therefore a mistake to assume a conflict between state interests and international law, and equally a mistake to see law as necessarily a constraint on anyone's agency. What counts as acting lawfully is often an open question, and states exploit this ambiguity to further their ends.

What is more, the normative bias in favor of compliance is politically naive, as it celebrates existing laws and institutions as manifestations of consensual cooperation rather than the global power game. As David Kennedy says, "Rather than seeing the hand of power in the glove of law, mainstream international lawyers focus on the glove."[41] Let us now remove the glove and consider the power within. I spend the next three chapters examining specific areas of legalized international politics: war, torture, and drones. These examples emphasize the limitations of the conventional approach I have criticized, showing how legalization empowers some actors and enervates others. Once we appreciate the breadth of uses to which legalization is put, and the range of its effects, we can turn to the system as a whole and consider the broad shape of its political and normative consequences.

4

The Permissive Power of the Ban on War

He who breaks the law has gone to war with the community; the community goes to war with him.

—FREDERICK POLLOCK AND FREDERIC WILLIAM MAITLAND, *THE HISTORY OF ENGLISH LAW*

This chapter takes the tools developed in chapter 3 to look at the use of international law around the regulation of war. The ban of war contained in the UN Charter is widely identified as central to the modern international order—Michael Byers calls it "one of the twentieth century's greatest achievements"—and it is often used as evidence of progress in world politics, an improvement on the "bad old days" when the decision to go to war was purely political and unconstrained by legal obligations.[1] Liberal internationalists suggest that these new laws contribute to a "cooperative rules-based order" by limiting the circumstances in which governments can go to war.[2] But the laws on war also do more than define which wars are unlawful. They also define other wars as lawful—specifically, wars of "self-defense"—and in doing so, create a situation in which states can gain political legitimation by presenting their recourse to war as motivated by self-defense. This is the permissive power of international law, and I explore it here and look also at ways that legality and state interests are closely connected in the practice of legal justification.

The rules on war have evolved since they were written for the UN Charter in 1945. State practice and interpretative trends have changed how the law is understood, and this change has mostly been in the direction of expanding the category of self-defense. Governments are freer to use force under the interpretation that prevails today than they would be if the rules were read in a more formal way as black-letter law. The distinction between lawful and unlawful war has shifted as a result of informal processes such that the law today cannot be known only by reference to its formal source. Since these processes are largely motivated by the acts and needs of strong states, the development of the law tends to follow the path that they set. Recognizing these processes takes us away from the classical model of law a set of regulative rules that limit state agency. In its place a dynamic and political model of law emerges—one that sees a recursive relationship among law, political power, and practices of legitimation. By defining what wars are lawful, and in bending to the changing interests of powerful states, the ban on war constitutes a resource that states use to legitimate their uses of force.

The chapter first looks at the legal rules that ban war by asking, What is it that states are required to do, and refrain from doing, in their use of force against other states? The UN Charter framework is anchored on three elements: that the threat or use of force by states is illegal, except when used for self-defense or as authorized by the UN Security Council. Global governance advocates frequently cite these components of the contemporary global order as essential. The first part of the chapter uses the conventional tools of legal interpretation to examine what these laws forbid, require, and permit. I pay particular attention to the role of "self-defense" in the legal regime on war and consider how it invites states' security "needs" into the determination of whether a war is lawful or not.

I then trace how the rules have been interpreted and applied in practice, focusing on the role of past practice and state interests in shaping how the law is understood. Debates over the meaning and application of the law frequently invoke past disputes, claims, and invocations as evidence, and also contend with competing claims about the "necessity" of war for self-defense. These changing interpretative resources have driven the contemporary content of the law away from its black-letter text. As state practice has changed what counts as lawful war, the change has a natural direction: it goes toward the desires of the most active agents. Over time, the rules move with the interests of those using the rules, and state interests become encoded inside "compliance" with the law. Following in the tradition of Kinsella, Harcourt, and others who study the history and dynamics of political distinctions, I consider how the distinction between compliance and noncompliance is constituted in part by these internalized interests.[3]

The final section considers the implications of that internalization. First, the legalization of war decisions after 1945 gives a legal basis for the pursuit of national security interests—it changes the politics of legitimation for war, but does not in itself speak to the frequency of war. Second, it shows the permissive function of international law, in the sense that it empowers governments to do some things as opposed to only preventing them from taking action. Third, the reflexive dynamic between legality and state interests makes the ban on war infrangible: if war is lawful when it serves the genuine security interests of the state, and states make their own judgments about the threats they face, then the ban on war has become "law that cannot be broken."

The Ban on War

The universal ban on interstate war is a central element of the UN Charter. For states that are members of the United Nations (which

THE PERMISSIVE POWER OF THE BAN ON WAR   61

today means all recognized states), it is illegal to use or threaten force against other states, except as necessary in self-defense to respond to an armed attack. This right expires once the Council has taken collective measures to restore international peace and security.

The key provision is Article 2(4) of the UN Charter. It says, "All members shall refrain in their international relations from the threat or use of force against the territorial integrity or political independence of any state, or in any other manner inconsistent with the Purposes of the United Nations."

This is supplemented by Article 51, which acknowledges the legality of war in self-defense:

> Nothing in the present Charter shall impair the inherent right of individual or collective self-defense if an armed attack occurs against a Member of the United Nations, until the Security Council has taken measures necessary to maintain international peace and security. Measures taken by Members in the exercise of this right of self-defense shall be immediately reported to the Security Council and shall not in any way affect the authority and responsibility of the Security Council under the present Charter to take at any time such action as it deems necessary in order to maintain or restore international peace and security.

The texts of Articles 2(4) and 51 are the foundation of the contemporary legal regime on war—the formal rules that distinguish acceptable from unacceptable uses of force. They embody the fundamental bargain in the post-1945 international security system: war decisions are made in the Security Council and are no longer the prerogative of individual governments.[4] The peace-and-security architecture of the UN system is the institutional expression of that premise. With these clauses, the Charter removes from states the right to decide as they wish how to use their militaries and installs in its place a collective system with the UN Security Council at the center.[5]

The attempt to regulate war through law and rules was not new in 1945; its first articulation as a legal obligation came in the Kellogg-Briand Pact of 1928, which was the first European treaty to outlaw war among its parties.[6] Before that, arguments about acceptable and unacceptable war were ancient.[7] The Charter, however, is remarkable for its turn to *law* and legal obligations that apply to all states in the international system. For the first time in the history of the Westphalian interstate system, war was made explicitly illegal for all states. The Charter subordinates national war decisions beneath a set of legal criteria that distinguish between legality and illegality in war making. It is novel both in its legalization and universality.[8]

The Ban on War as the Start of Global Order

For many authors, the introduction of law into the decision to go to war marks a dramatic break in the management of international affairs, in Europe and beyond. It is often used as evidence that the post-1945 world is fundamentally different from what existed before. For instance, according to Tom Ruys, "Up until the end of the nineteenth century, the predominant conviction was that every State had a customary right, inherent in sovereignty itself, to embark upon war whenever it pleased."[9] This right was activated when a sovereign claimed to have experienced harm at the hands of a foreign agent. The pre-1945 discourse of war legitimation emphasized the existence of such harm and the legitimacy of the use of force in response.[10] Precipitating harms might include unpaid debts, territorial incursion, dynastic disputes, regional destabilization, and more, and the actors perpetrating those harms might include other sovereigns, their diplomats and agents, or even firms and individuals.[11] Thus, war choices in the eighteenth- and nineteenth-century European system were legitimated in political rather than legal terms.[12]

By imposing a legal framework on war, the UN Charter ended this era. In its place, Christine Gray says the Charter "provides a new terminology and the first expression of the basic rules [for war] in their modern form."[13] Byers sees this as "a constitutional moment in international affairs: an anarchic world of self-help and temporary alliances was transformed into a nascent system of governance."[14] Franck maintains that it launched the modern age, distinguished by the "idea that the use of force by a state against another could itself be violative of the legal order's very foundations."[15]

This argument is often derided as "world peace through world law."[16] But its central insight—that rules organize world politics toward order—has been adopted widely by liberal, realist, and many critical writers across political science, history, and legal theory. For instance, Hedley Bull identified rules on violence as a key component of the existence of society itself, whether domestic or international. Society, for Bull, begins when individuals put aside their natural right to act as they see fit, and become both encumbered and liberated by rules that constrain their recourse to violence.[17] International society is therefore inconceivable without rules that regulate war. International law scholars often arrive at the same conclusion but by starting at a different point: regulating interstate war is the paradigmatic, essential task of public international law; it is common among international lawyers to equate international law with the regulation of violence itself. Hersch Lauterpacht notes that the "primordial duty of the [international] law" is to enact the rule that "there shall be no violence" by states.[18] O'Connell says that "law is valued for providing an alternative to the use of force in the ordering of human affairs. In this sense, all of international law is law of peace."[19] For Lauterpacht, as for O'Connell, the regulation of war is inseparable from the concept of public international law itself.[20] Both also share with Bull the faith that controlling war with law will allow international society to emerge among nations.

Ikenberry provides a defense of the view that international rules and institutions, the ban on war prominent among them, are the foundation of contemporary order. For Ikenberry, the post-1945 world is characterized by the multilateral commitment to a rules-based international system. In this "liberal hegemonic order," the commitment to international legal institutions creates

> an order where weaker states participate willingly—rather than resist of balance against the leading power. . . . Weaker states agree to the order's rules and institutions, and in return they are assured that the worst excesses of the leading state— manifesting as arbitrary and indiscriminate abuses of power— will be avoided, and they gain institutional opportunities to work and help influence the leading state.[21]

Ikenberry is expressing the intuition behind liberal internationalism more generally when he says that the rules and institutions that make up the international order increase the security of both strong and weak states, and thus should gain the consent of these states.

> The United States built postwar order within the Western world—and extending outward—on liberal ideas and principles . . . looking after the overall stability and openness of the system. . . . In ideal form, liberal international order is sustained through consent rather than balance or command. States voluntarily join the order and operate within it according to mutually agreed-on rules and arrangements. The rule of law, rather than crude power politics, is the framework of interstate relations.[22]

In such a system, "power is exercised through sponsorship of rules and institutions," Ikenberry adds.[23] The progress of "liberal" postwar settlements since 1815 has therefore been "based on a set of principles of restraint and accommodation," anchored by limitations on interstate violence.[24]

It isn't only liberals such as Ikenberry who see the ban on war as the structure for interstate politics. Henry Nau, promoting what he calls "conservative internationalism," takes a similar view, although he limits its scope to "the West." In that region (or perhaps a "community"), he sees a unified international identity "in which common law and institutions replace the balance of power and anarchy."[25] He differentiates his view from that of the liberals by explicitly endorsing the use of force as a means to expand the reach of that identity, asserting that "given the continuing range of threats, the use of force to promote a freedom-forward diplomacy persists."[26] Nau never accounts for what "freedom" means, nor does he show any connection between it and US military operations, and as a consequence his policy prescriptions carry little weight—but he shares with Ikenberry and others the view that international rules take the place of power politics, and hence contribute to international order.

A version of this commitment, albeit with a different political valence, appears also in the work Michael Hardt and Antonio Negri. In identifying global power in late modernity, Hardt and Negri find an emerging "imperial sovereignty . . . an imperial notion of right" that straddles the conventional divides of domestic/international and public/private power. The "juridification" of global power has reconstituted sovereign authority in a constellation of institutions and practices across these divides, creating "a machine that imposes procedures of continual contractualization that lead to systemic equilibria"—in other words, a codification of states' and subjects' legal obligations along with the repackaging of their political relations in legal terms.[27] This is echoed in B. S. Chimni's account of the "emerging global state" that he sees arising in the form of the interconnected web of international political, legal, and economic institutions.[28]

Hardt and Negri identify the ban on war and legalization of war in the United Nations as the mid-twentieth-century hallmarks of the juridification of politics, both global and local: the reconstitution of war as a specifically *legal* category produces "the right of duty of the dominant subjects of the world order to intervene in the territories of other subjects in the interest of preventing or resolving humanitarian problems, guaranteeing accords, and imposing peace." This juridical global power they call "Empire." As they contend, "Empire is not born of its own will but rather it is *called* into being and constituted on the basis of its capacity to resolve conflicts. Empire is formed and its intervention becomes juridically legitimate only when it is already inserted into the chain of international consensus aimed at resolving existing conflicts."[29] For Hardt and Negri, the turn to law to adjudicate international disputes and decide when war is permitted constitutes Empire as an emerging form of global sovereignty.

From O'Connell to Nau to Hardt and Negri, there is a widespread commitment to the view that the legalization of war decisions in the mid-twentieth century makes a crucial contribution to the contemporary international order. It gives a specifically legal frame to the distinction between legitimate and illegitimate wars, and organizes international political power in ways that would seem alien to the nineteenth-century model of diplomatic accommodation in European power politics.[30] By setting *legal* criteria that differentiate legitimate from illegitimate wars, the new system invites competing claims regarding the relevant laws and their application to particular circumstances. This gives rise to familiar debates about how the rules should be interpreted and applied, which I discuss next, but the point of the present section is that these debates take place within a shared commitment to the ideas that in principle, states' uses of force can be divided into legal and illegal, and the UN Charter and other texts provide the resources for making that distinction.

The Interpretation of 2(4): Text and Practice

What, then, is allowed under the rules, and what is forbidden? This section considers what it means to comply with the ban on war. The conventional account of the international rule of law is that the law should clearly distinguish lawful from unlawful conduct by states, and separate compliance from noncompliance. With this distinction somewhat stable, the behavioral effect of the law comes from its ability to give rewards to those who comply and punishments to those who do not.[31] As we will see, things are more complicated in practice, but in the case of the ban on war this ideal-type provides a useful baseline for considering how international law in fact relates to international politics in the real world.

The primary source for determining the legality of war is the UN Charter. In the hierarchy of sources of international law, a treaty is understood to supply the strongest evidence for the existence of a legal rule, and therefore much has been invested in parsing its clauses on war.[32] The standard doctrine of international legal interpretation says this should be guided by the "ordinary meaning of the terms" in the treaty.[33] For the legality of war, the Charter clearly permits the use force only in response to an armed attack or as authorized by the UN Security Council.

This is the textual foundation for law against war. It appears regularly in the justifications states use to argue for their wars. It was invoked, for instance, by the United Kingdom in relation to its military action against Argentina's occupation of the Falkland Islands in 1982; when diplomatic negotiation and then Security Council Resolution 502 did not lead to Argentina's withdrawal, the government of Margaret Thatcher used its military to achieve that result by force.[34] In 1990, self-defense was the legal rationale that permitted international military intervention to repel the Iraqi Army from Kuwait. In that case, it was used by the UN Security Council to affirm "the inherent right of individual or collective self-defence, in response to the armed attack by Iraq against Kuwait." This situated the US-led coalition against Iraq within the legal framework of self-defense in the UN Charter.[35] By contrast, when the United States and others invaded Iraq in 2003, there was no plausible way to frame it as self-defense. The United States instead made an unconvincing appeal back to the 1990 resolutions and was widely condemned for violating the laws on war in the process.[36]

The Charter provides the first word on the subject of lawful war, but it is rarely allowed the last word, and the Iraq 2003 example hints at why.[37] The key phrases in the law (armed attack, use of force, and the purposes of the United Nations, among others) require interpretation, and there is ample space within them for competing interpretations of both the law and facts of the situation to which they are applied. These interpretative controversies are well known.[38] They include questions such as whether the "threat or use of force" includes nonmilitary forms of coercion such as embargoes, market pressure, and diplomatic sanctions; whether it prohibits attacks on private as opposed to governmental targets in other countries; whether it permits attacks on a government if the provoking act originated with a nonstate actor and not the state; whether the phrase "the territorial or political independence" narrows or merely illustrates the scope of what is forbidden; and what is meant by "or any other manner that is inconsistent with the purposes of the United Nations."

In interpreting the meaning of the formal language, two sets of resources do most of the work: those historical instances in which governments have invoked and argued over the meaning of the law in the past, and the plausibility of the state's claim to self-defense. I examine next how these two constitute the contemporary ban on war, and are integral to assessing the legality and illegality of uses of force. Together they also allow the self-identified security interests of states to determine the legality of their actions and so make legality derivative of those interests rather than a source of external judgment of state action.

State Practice in the Interpretation of the Ban on War

How the rules have been used, interpreted, and argued over in past practice is significant for resolving ambiguity as well as filling lacunae in international law. According to Franck, state practice gives " 'live' meaning . . . to inert words by existential experience and transactional processes."[39] It is taken as evidence of how governments understand the content of their obligations, and thus what they consider to be lawful and unlawful.[40] This is implied by the logic of consent and obligation at the heart of international law itself: since states are the agents that consent to the obligations in the treaty, their own understanding of the content of those obligations is relevant when resolving controversies around them.

Past practice toward a piece of international law can change the meaning of the obligations that it contains—indeed it must, since unless it can do so, there is no point in consulting practice as a means to understand the text. As illustrations, Franck notes several areas in which the obligations of state toward the ban on war have changed since 1945 despite no change in the Charter language. Article 51, for example, establishes that states must cease their "self-defense" operations when the Security Council takes action on the matter. This has not been followed in practice, and international judicial and political institutions have endorsed this failure as legally adequate.[41]

More consequential for international politics is the expansion of "anticipatory" self-defense. The Charter formally outlaws such action: it requires that "an armed attack has occurred" before self-defense is permitted. But the rule has been read almost from the start as permitting some anticipatory wars, and the legality of the practice is in principle widely accepted.[42] The controversy over anticipation comes from disagreement over how to identify the *circumstances* in which it is legal, and on this the most common formulation invokes the *Caroline* case from 1837 to find that anticipatory attacks are lawful when the threat of attack is "imminent."[43]

Scholars and states have reconciled this practical reading of the law with its more restrictive Charter text in two ways: by suggesting that anticipatory self-defense is part of the "inherent" right to self-defense that the Charter "shall not impair," and by showing that the practical implications of banning anticipatory war are unworkable and thus the Charter cannot possibly mean what it says. The first is a technical legal argument, and the second a consequentialist one, but they lead to the same outcome: the use of force prior to an armed attack is presented as lawful despite the plain text of the Charter as well as its *traveaux preparatoires*.[44]

The "adaptability" of the Charter to new situations is widely accepted by governments and scholars. It isn't particularly controversial.[45] It presumes that the line separating acceptable from unacceptable behavior is not clear or fixed, and that past state practice can illuminate where the line lies today. Many scholars see this as a desirable feature of international law, as does Franck, who says that a "strictly literal interpretation of the Charter's collective security system" became "unworkable" after 1945 and so its interpretative expansion since then has been a good thing.[46] W. Michael Reisman argues against having international rules that are "mechanically applied"—after all, he observes, the "political [and] technological environment have been changing inexorably since the end of the 19th century," and our reading of the law must change with it. To do otherwise he adds (in a startling choice of phrase), "rapes common sense."[47] The interpretation of a treaty must keep up with "evolutions in the international security environment," and remain "in accord with changing circumstances and social values."[48] Byers says it is "a pragmatic response" of law to the present needs of states.[49] Ruys notes that "legal rules are not static, but are capable of evolving over time."[50]

The implication of this flexibility is that the legal status of an act may change even if the text of the law has not. What was legal may become illegal, and vice versa, in response to certain changes in the external environment such as in military technology, the nature of threats, and consequent changes in the needs of states for defense against them. Legal interpretations that are "not evident from the text" (in Franck's words) sometimes come to be accepted as authoritative, at which point legality no longer means being faithful to the language of the treaty.[51] According to Reisman, "One should not seek point-for-point conformity to a rule without constant regard for the policy or principle that animated its prescription."[52] Jan Klabbers remarks that "many possibly illegal acts have been warmly welcomed by the membership of the organization concerned, ranging from usurpation of powers to debatable use of credentials procedures. In turn, this creates the following situation: if a healthy majority agrees with the activity, then it can hardly be deemed illegal, for, if it were illegal, how could a healthy majority possibly accept it?"[53] To the extent that the law is specified by reference to how it has been used in the past, then possibly illegal acts can be reconstituted as legal depending on how they are received by the society. These "uses of history" ensure that the law is not seriously at odds with the interests of powerful actors.[54] The dynamics of legal development work toward the natural and perpetual coincidence of law and great power interests.

The "Self" in Self-Defense

The Charter creates a legal regime in which self-defense is the sole lawful motivation for a state using force outside its borders. This is what Schachter called "defensism" with respect to the laws on war—where the needs of self-defense define the outer bounds of legality.[55] As mentioned above, this has come to be understood to include the use of force before an armed attack has occurred as long as it responds to an imminent threat of attack. Defensism as a legal justification suggests that states act legally (and rightly) when they respond militarily to the "compulsion from fear" produced by an external threat.[56]

It is not surprising, then, that self-defense has become the most popular justification for war, often with all sides in the conflict claiming it as their motivation. In debates about the appropriate application of the law and its core concept, most attention has focused on what might be called the "genuineness" of the connection between the use of force and security needs of the state; for instance, the *Nicaragua* decision at the ICJ was founded on the Court's rejection of "justification of collective self-defense maintained by the United States in connection with the military and paramilitary activities in and against Nicaragua."[57] To make a judgment about whether the use of force is "necessary" for a state's self-defense requires assessing the security needs of the state as well as the nature, imminence, and other qualities of the external threat, and also the utility and proportionality of military force in remedying the threat.[58] These questions open the space for disagreement and controversy that characterizes the history of claims to self-defense under international law. For methodological positivist approaches to international law, resolving these questions is crucial since only by that path can one determine when states are complying with or violating the law. Postpositivist approaches are not committed to finding answers to such questions, and instead see them as reflecting political disagreements about what the rules should be, what conduct should be sanctioned, and in what way.

The concept of self-defense also presumes an understanding of what constitutes the self that states have a right to defend. On this issue, the direction of state practice since 1945 has been remarkably consistent: the self is expanding. The self in self-defense has grown beyond the territorial borders of the state and now encompasses a range of state interests abroad. This is despite no change in the underlying formal texts. For instance, citizens abroad are now often invoked as the subjects of self-defense—Entebbe being the classic example, but many states have made similar operations and justifications.[59] Similarly, the US legal justification for its drone policy asserts that self-defense authorizes the United States to kill people anywhere in the world who are affiliated with "al Qaeda and associated forces," and who cannot be captured.[60] In the Cold War, both the United States and Soviet Union invoked self-defense to justify military operations designed to install or maintain governments that were consistent with their spheres of influence, on the theory that any adverse change of government was likely the result of "external aggression."[61] More recently, the North Atlantic Treaty Organization has taken on an active military role outside the territory of its members, in Bosnia, Kosovo, Afghanistan, and Libya, with the justification that its defensive phi-

losophy has "move[d] from a geographical to a functional understanding of security."[62] In other words, the self that it defends is
conceptual rather than territorial; it is the sum of the national
interests of its members. Threats to the self might therefore emanate from other states (say, Kuwait's response to the Iraq invasion
in 1990) and entities other than states (the United States and others
in Afghanistan and elsewhere from 2001 on).

Many of these uses of the law are highly contentious among
legal scholars, but they reflect the political power of international
legal justification. These are the terms in which states argue for
the legitimacy of their wars, and they presume a confidence on
the part of the state that the language of self-defense provides
political support for war in a way that its absence does not. Just as
the concepts of the "civilian" and its opposite are key to defining
what is an acceptable target in armed conflict, the concept of self-
defense is accepted as the key to differentiating between acceptable and unacceptable uses of force.[63] Kinsella shows for the civil-
ian/combatant dichotomy how the distinction is politically
powerful even when there is controversy or uncertainty about
who resides on which side of the line. For self-defense, the power
of the concept to legitimize war is not dependent on there being
a consensus over what precisely it means. Claims about self-
defense are appeals for political legitimation for war, making use
of interpretative resources and understandings already existing in
interstate relations.

The contemporary expansive understanding of self-defense
in effect substitutes "threat" as the trigger for military response
where the Charter text says "armed attack." Self-defense has come
to refer to the defense of the interests of the state, not of its physical
borders and territory. Operationalized this way, the rule gives
states a right to use force to change circumstances abroad that it
deems unfavorable to its national security and thus permits a much
wider range of uses of force than the literal reading of the Charter
would suggest.[64] It makes a "threat to the self" a sufficient provoca-
tion to authorize a military response. It also draws a circle back to

the nineteenth-century model of war as a response to harm: self-defense in response to a threat to national interests is indistinguishable from a model that legitimates war in response to the harms suffered by the sovereign. The justification is now in legal as opposed to political terms, but its relation to the sovereign and the sovereign's interests is unchanged.

When put together with the expansion of self-defense to include acts taken before "an armed attack occurs," the result is that state practice under the UN Charter has loosened the restrictions of war in both time and space. Lawful self-defense can now apparently take place before or long after an armed attack. This eliminates the limit implied by *ratione tempori*.[65] It can also take place against nonstate actors or in defense of citizens abroad. This eliminates the state-centric limit on *ratione personae*. Self-defense has lost both its physical and temporal limits. This vastly widens the possibility for international military conflict that is seen as lawful under the Charter, and makes the ban on war look more like an authorization of force than a constraint on it.[66]

To sum up, the ban on war has evolved under the influence of state practice, especially the practice of strong states, and self-defense has come to dominate the process of assessing the legality of the use of force by states. Both developments make it more difficult for states to violate the law against war, as their own interests are already incorporated into the meaning of compliance. Compliance is increasingly guaranteed by the mutual implication of law and interests.

This does not suggest that anything states want to do can be made lawful just by their making a claim to that effect. Governments and others deploy claims about legality in the pursuit of legitimation. These claims are often highly contested by both legal specialists who might object to how the law is being characterized and political actors who object to the actions being legitimated by the claims. For example, the question of whether US attacks against the Islamic State of Iraq and the Levant in Syria since 2016 *really are* self-defense or not under the UN Charter is not likely to be resolved; the issue rests on controversies over what the law allows and forbids as well as how these US actions fit into the law, and on these points it is probably unrealistic to expect convergence on any settled consensus. Regardless of the controversy, however, it is clear that in this instance, the United States desires to be seen as acting lawfully, and this desire reflects political power that comes from the international rule of law as an ideology. Governments are motivated to fit themselves into the confines of international legality because it brings them political legitimation. This is the heart of the international rule of law.

The permissive power of international law also implies constraints. I have focused on the permissive side here as I think this is frequently overlooked, but constraints from law are important as well. Both a general and specific form of constraint is worth considering: first, the need for legal justification is a kind of general constraint on governments in that the desire for legal legitimation makes it more difficult to take actions for which legal justifications are hard to find; and second, for the ban on war, the Charter clearly outlaws wars that are not motivated by self-defense, and so makes it more difficult for states to engage in wars of aggression, profit, humanitarianism, and other motives.

My goal is to highlight the political power of these legal claims. The contestation over the meaning and application of legal resources is itself evidence of the importance of international law and legality in global politics. This leads to the *opposite* conclusion than that drawn by some IR realists who suggest that international law is relatively unimportant in power politics. I show instead that the permissive power of international law is of central significance to governments: legality, when it lines up with state interests, enhances state power and governments make use of it in the pursuit of this power. This perspective connects political power and the international rule of law in a manner that is more realistic than that of the self-styled realists in IR theory.

Implications

The UN Charter does not outlaw war. Instead, it changes the categories under which war may be lawfully pursed by states. The difference is significant, both conceptually and substantively, for the study of international law and politics. First, it means that the difference between pre- and post-1945 lies in the social framework of political legitimation through law rather than in the legal status of war as such. Self-defense has been institutionalized as a legitimate justification for war. Second, it gives states a new justification for war (that is, self-defense) and this is a permissive as opposed to constraining force. It makes the choice to use force *easier* for states rather than harder. It reinforces the fact that there is no reason to expect the incidence of war to decline after 1945; what we should expect to see is a change in the justifications that states use for war, and this we do indeed see. Finally, the merger of law and state interests means that the conceptual distinction between "following the law" and "following interests" has been eliminated. This undermines both the rationalist method of studying the impact of international law and positivist attempt to measure compliance with it.[67]

WHAT CHANGED AS A RESULT OF THE CHARTER?

This difference between the pre-1945 world and the world of the UN Charter is frequently misspecified. Those who see the ban on war in 1945 as a "transformative moment in international affairs" and "radical departure in the systemic response to violence among states," see the laws against war as a constraint on states agency. In this view, the Charter is a new external obstacle to states' pursuit of what they see as their interests with respect to war; it suggests that the power of the rules is manifest when states choose to follow the rules (and refrain from the use of force) rather than follow their independent interests, which might be driving them to war. What is new, in that model, is that the illegality of war makes war harder to choose.

The evidence in this chapter suggests a different interpretation of the change brought about by the Charter. Rather than outlaw war, it is more accurate to say that the Charter changed the terms of political legitimation for states engaging in war. It differentiates among the purposes for war, and makes some purposes more legitimate and others less. Specifically, it gives privileged status to self-defense and forbids all other purposes. This is not a comprehensive ban on war, and its success cannot be measured by a decline in the incidence of war overall. The change is in what Raz calls the lawful "reason for action."[68] Its impact therefore should be evident in whether and how this new resource is or is not taken up and used by actors. By this test, the Charter rules on war are enormously successful, as self-defense and Article 51 have become ubiquitous in states' justifications for military action, and the pre-1945 justifications have almost disappeared. It is another question altogether whether this is a step forward or backward for the substantive goals of national, international, or human security. In this light, the main challenge to the laws comes from novel claims that there may exist legal justifications for war outside the framework of Articles 51 and 2(4); there are several candidates in this category, including humanitarian intervention, responsibility to protect, the defense of democracy, and more, though it is telling that the strongest arguments for each of these fall short of suggesting they are lawful in a formal sense in international law.[69]

PERMISSIVE LAW

As I suggested in chapter 3, action is only possible when the actor has access to reasons and meaning that situate their action in its social context. This is a central tenet of a pragmatic approach to social theory from Charles Taylor and others, where a shared understanding of the meaning of certain kinds of acts is a precondition for meaningful action.[70] To sign a contract, vote in an election, or walk a picket line depends on an existing framework of social understandings that make it possible for the actor to engage in the action, and without such a framework the acts are impossible. One cannot do what one cannot conceive, at least not intentionally. The invention of new social categories thus makes new kinds of action possible, as with civil unions, "stand your ground," or wars of self-defense. The addition expands the set of options available for agents to choose.

Martha Finnemore has explored this phenomenon with respect to the invention of "humanitarian intervention" as a kind of military action.[71] Beginning in the 1980s, as humanitarian intervention came to be widely understood as a distinct and potentially legitimate use of force by states, governments could do something that they literally could not do before. Finnemore argues that in the process, states gained a policy option that they previously did not have and became empowered in a way that would not have made sense at the start of the twentieth century. State power increased as a result (at least for some states).

The Charter forbids wars that are not essential for national security, and this outlaws wars of aggression, retaliation, colonialism, honor, and profit. No state today claims these are the motive for their wars. This is persuasive evidence of the success of the law. But the Charter legitimates defensive wars, and as such, after the Charter states have in self-defense a justification for military action that is endorsed by the political power of international legalization. It is no surprise that states have been enthusiastic about identifying their wars as defensive. This points to the permissive power of the law on war: to go ahead with a war, states are encouraged to explain how it qualifies as self-defense, which means showing how it serves the essential security interests of the state. Failing to this incentive raises the costs of war for governments, in much the same way that Waltz suggested that states are induced to follow other structural incentives in the international system such as self-help.[72]

INFRANGIBLE LAW

Scholars may well strive to identify a conceptual core to the idea of self-defense, but few real-world instances where the concept is invoked are so clear-cut; it is likely that all such claims are contested. These dynamics account for the characteristic controversies that accompany claims to self-defense, as when one's opponent challenges the authenticity of the claim. The typical result is that the parties advance competing interpretations of the facts of the case, security needs of the actors, and law itself in support of their preferred policy positions. Many scholars interpret such disputes as a sign of a problem for the law and perhaps even evidence of desuetude; in 1970 Franck declared Article 2(4) "dead" from gross misuse and misinterpretation, and Michael Glennon updated that claim in the 2000s.[73] But this conclusion mistakes manipulation for disregard; it treats the law as a regulative rule rather than a resource of legitimation. States work hard to remain within the limits provided by international law, and part of this effort is evident in their provision of explanations about their behavior as well as the congruence between their behavior and for the law. The utility that actors find in invoking the rules to explain their actions is evidence of both law's malleability and its continuing, compelling political appeal. These suggest that the law is highly salient to actors, which is the *opposite* of desuetude.

States' ability to use the self to redefine the law in line with their national security interests leads not to desuetude but rather to infrangibility. An infrangible law is one that cannot be broken, and the ban on war's internalization of state interests produces this effect. As long as states are using war only to secure their own selves, then their actions cannot be violations of Articles 51 and 2(4). The Charter is automatically complied with in the course of pursuing the state's self-understood, national security self-interest. The appropriateness of claims to self-defense is established when the state is genuinely defending its essential needs in response to an external threat. Thus, to delegitimate a claim to self-defense requires providing an account of the state's interests that denies that the war was in fact necessary for the country's security.

The legalization of self-defense provides a novel institutional home for the old concept of *raisons d'état* as justification for war. Where in earlier periods these *raisons* might take the form of the needs of the sovereign in relation to harms caused by outsiders, in our current legalized period they are defined in relation to threats to the national security of the state. International legalization has rewritten "just war theory" as "legal war theory." Niccolò Machiavelli said "that war is just which is necessary."[74] In light of the Charter, today he could say "that war is legal which is necessary."

Conclusion

The ban on war has been remade since 1945 by the influence of state practice. It has been reconstituted through its use such that its content continuously reflects what Karl Marx called "the struggles and wishes of the age."[75] The literal reading of the Charter has never been taken seriously as the operative rules on war, but law has not been abandoned. States and others remain committed to the premise that the use of force should follow international law— that is, to the international rule of law understood as compliance. What has changed in this formula is what compliance with the law entails.

Many have tried to understand what Reisman called the "curious legal grey area [that] extended between the black letter of the Charter and the bloody reality of world politics."[76] Most often, the proposed solution involves searching for more precision in the law itself, on the faith that by logical and historical inquiry, one can identify what is and is not permitted under the law. Ruys argues that "the confusion on the shared normative framework renders it increasingly difficult to come to a reasoned consensus on the legality of a particular intervention through the exchange of claims and counter-claims at the international level. The implication is an erosion of the 'compliance pull' of the *Ius ad Bel-*

lum, which can only be remedied by a much-needed clarification of the law."[77]

Instead, I suggest that the legal regime around the use of force can better be understood as a practice rather than as a fixed distinction between legal and illegal acts. The ban on war provides resources with which states strive to legitimize their international uses of force. It does not give a fixed, objective standard by which conduct can be judged to be either lawful or unlawful. As a consequence, compliance with the law on war comes to look like a derivative of state interests as opposed to standing independent of them. And the law may perhaps contribute to international order, yet it does not do so by holding firm the line against inter-state "aggression." Instead, it legitimates state behavior by legalizing it, making certain categories of war more rather than less possible.

This complicates the conventional liberal contention that controlling violence is the central purpose of international law, as is on display when Byers says that "to improve the world—for everyone . . . obeying the requirements of war law is a necessary first step."[78] Instead, obeying the law as set out in Articles 2(4) and 51 leads to a more nuanced set of outcomes. Following the law is not distinct from states' following their security self-interests, and the change in the legal justification for war says nothing about the frequency with which states might use military force. The ban on war creates a legal circularity that enables states to use force within the political structure of international law. It constitutes a legalized system of raisons d'etat at the heart of the modern legal-political system, and what it means to comply with the law is not independent of what governments want to do: legality is a function of state interests.

5

The Rule of No Law

NUKES, DRONES, AND
THE HORROR VACUI

> Since the mid-twentieth century, there are no more legal
> black holes on Earth.
> —HAUKE BRUNKHORST, *CRITICAL THEORY OF LEGAL*
> *REVOLUTIONS: EVOLUTIONARY PERSPECTIVES*

> It is the considered view of this Administration . . . that
> the US targeting practices, including lethal operations
> conducted with the use of unmanned aerial vehicles, comply
> with all applicable law, including the law of war.
> —HAROLD KOH, LEGAL ADVISER FOR THE
> US DEPARTMENT OF STATE

In this chapter, I examine the political power of legalization in
situations where there is no international law. I look for what exists beyond the outer edge of international legalization, in the
policy space before it is "legalized," by exploring two cases where
new technologies make possible new kinds of behavior by governments. Novel practices by definition have not yet been brought

THE RULE OF NO LAW 83

into the legal framework through a treaty or other means. I am interested in the difference between legalized policy choices and their prelegal antecedents. The standard model of law presumes a stark difference between the two; it is often seen as the difference between the rule of law and unmitigated coercion. But I find something else. In the cases I examine, the newly available policy options are interpreted as already within international legal categories. They do not arise in a legal void where states' underlying free will is unfettered. The practices of international law fill these ostensibly prelegal spaces even without a process of legalization. The gaps disappear as if by a force of nature, a legalist *horro vacui*. By this process, the permissive and constraining effects of international law are evident in both the pre- and postlegalization worlds, and the sharp distinction between the two conditions is erased.

The power of the international rule of law when there is no law is something of a strange concept but it has in fact been in front of scholars and practitioners for a long time. It is present, for instance, in thinking about the legal obligations of states in the "state of nature," the possibility and implication of gaps in international legalization, and formalism and its alternatives in legal scholarship.[1] It is at the heart of debates around natural law, *jus cogens*, legal lacunae, the completeness of law, the *Lotus* decision, non liquet, and other concepts central to the international legal system. Among political scientists, it also often appears as a point of reference to which the postlegalization political order is compared: legalization is said to be important because it brings legal resources to the nonlegal relations that existed before. It points toward a temporal sequence in which a "no-law" condition existed prior to the advent of legal resources and was replaced by legalization. In this sense, the international rule of law depends on the existence of gaps in legal coverage.

This chapter shows something different: governments invoke legal understandings for even novel policy problems and so legal gaps are filled as quickly as they are discovered. Legal "black holes" might exist in positive law, but the political uses of law fill them in. The use of legal arguments to legitimize government choices does not wait for a formal transition from a prelegal to a legalized condition; legal resources fill a gap when a motivated actor advances legal arguments that frame obligations and responsibilities using legal resources.

The invention of new weapons technologies provides a natural location to study the politics of law by giving a view into what happens in the absence of law. New inventions make possible the kinds of actions that were likely not envisioned by the laws of the past. They prima facia exist in gaps in the law, and this no-law position can help illuminate how the addition of international law changes the situation. In this chapter, I use the cases of nuclear weapons and armed drones to explore two such instances in world politics. With nuclear weapons in the twentieth century and drones in the twenty-first, states and their advisers were confronted with policy possibilities that were not foreseen by the then-existing international rules on warfare. Both cases were attended by active debate about how the new technologies would fit into the existing scheme of lawful and unlawful state acts. One possible answer is that until a new treaty or custom is agreed to, governments are entirely free to use the new weapons as they wish. This suits how many scholars describe the state of affairs prior to the advent of international legalization; Goldstein and colleagues, for instance, say that states' "autonomy would be less constrained" before legalization as opposed to after, and Terence Halliday and Gregory Shaffer suggest that a "transnational legal order" is an effort "to produce some order out of chaos, anarchy, unpredictability, or irregularity."[2] This view was advanced with respect to nuclear weapons by one judge at the International Court of Justice (ICJ), but his colleagues rejected it; it hasn't received much support with respect to armed drones either. The more popular view is that old rules apply to the new weapons, albeit with various interpretative and political amendments along the way updating them in accord with the desires of the strong states. This implies that the new practices arrive into an already-legalized terrain rather than outside the legal order. It contradicts the conventional, temporal understanding of a sequence from a prelegalized world to a world with law. In its place, it shows that law and legalization pervades international politics today. It is inescapable and authoritative, which leads in chapter 7 to my conclusion that contemporary international affairs takes place within an "empire of legalism."

Law and No Law: Nukes

The *Nuclear Weapons* advisory opinion provides some resources for thinking about how international law and politics fit into potential gaps in the law. In the 1990s, the ICJ was asked the following question: "Is the threat or use of nuclear weapons in any circumstances permitted under international law?"[3] This arose from the rules in the ICJ Statute that permit international organizations to ask the ICJ for an opinion on some question of international law. The advisory opinions that it provides are nonbinding on governments, and their impact, if any, comes from the political and legal weight of the Court itself. On nuclear weapons, the Court's opinion included three components: it separated questions about how nuclear weapons might be used from questions about the legality of the weapons in themselves; it noted an abundance of legal resources on the former and the complete absence on the latter; and it produced two competing claims about how, given that absence, the legality of the weapons should be determined.

The standard doctrine on sources of international law says that treaties have priority over all other kinds of law. The ICJ judges therefore began by considering whether there are treaties that speak to the legality of nuclear weapons. It found none. While various instruments do create certain obligations toward nuclear weapons and their use, including the Non-Proliferation Treaty, treaties on nuclear-free zones, and various laws of armed conflict, there is no general statement anywhere in international law that defines nuclear weapons as either prohibited or permitted. The Court therefore concluded that on the issue of the legality of the weapons as such, "there is in neither customary nor conventional international law any specific authorization of the threat or use of nuclear weapons." Equally, it said, there are no positive legal resources that create "any comprehensive and universal prohibition of the threat or use of nuclear weapons as such." The closest it could get to finding them illegal was when it observed that given the widespread damage likely to follow from nuclear weapon use, "the use of such weapons in fact seems scarcely reconcilable with" the obligation to avoid harm to civilians.[4] But this was not enough to render them inherently illegal. They then considered whether customary law contained any such rules and again failed to find anything that was generally accepted by states as legally binding custom regarding nuclear weapons. They found therefore that the legality of nuclear weapons per se could not be either established or contradicted by reference to international law alone.

At this point, the judges are close to a paradigm case of non liquet—that is, finding that the question cannot be answered because no law exists to answer it. The concept is rarely used—indeed, it is forbidden in many international tribunals—but it is extremely important as a conceptual category because it marks the outer edge of international legalization.[5] It may also hint at what lies beyond it. Aznar-Gomez defines non liquet as "the nonsolution of a dispute [by a court] due to the absence of an applicable rule."[6] Ilmar Tammelo illustrates non liquet by the analogy with the game of chess before the invention of stalemate in the nineteenth century; before that, the rules simply did not say what should happen when the side to move is not in check but cannot make a legal move.[7]

The concept of non liquet presumes a positivist idea of international law in the sense of a set of rules that are brought into being by the consent of states. This perspective accepts that the international legal system is a patchwork of legalized and nonlegalized areas: where states have consented to rules they are bound by international law, and where they have not consented there is a gap in legal coverage. It is described as an "incomplete" system.[8] There are gaps where states have not yet consented to legal rules. This might cover an entire policy area (say, hunting whales before the advent of the International Convention on the Regulation of Whaling) or only one state (Russian whaling is not covered by those rules because it has withdrawn from the convention). The gaps could in principle be filled in as governments negotiate and accept new treaties and other rules. The "progressive" idea of international law described in chapter 2 presumes that expanding the domain of law (and thus shrinking the domain of no law) is in itself a worthy contribution in international affairs.

If one believes that international law has such gaps, then it becomes important to figure out what are the obligations of governments when they act in those spaces. When making a policy decision in a gap, how do governments relate to international law, if at all? The classical answer, from the *Lotus* decision of 1926, is that where no law exists states are free to act as they wish. This originates with a case at the ICJ's predecessor, the Permanent Court of International Justice, which was asked whether Turkey had acted unlawfully in arresting a French national for acts on the high seas that caused harm to Turkish interests. The Permanent Court of International Justice decided that Turkey was within its rights because there was no clear law to forbid its action.[9] It attached this finding to a broad statement about the relation between state sovereignty and international law:

> International law governs relations between independent States. The rules of law binding upon States therefore emanate from their own free will as expressed in conventions or by usages generally accepted as expressing principles of law and established in order to regulate the relations between these co-existing independent communities or with a view to the achievement of common aims. Restrictions upon the independence of States cannot therefore be presumed.[10]

This has become the iconic statement of what J.P.A. François called the "legal vacuum theory," which says that "if there is an occurrence that is not covered by existing international law, then the State affected by this transpiration is free to formulate rules to meet the problems thus created."[11] It reflects a liberal social-contract view of international legalization, in which the actor's free will brings into being the constraints on it that make society possible. John Bolton has said that "the central philosophical question about 'international law' is a liberty issue: How does this corpus of 'law' affect individuals in the exercise of their individual freedom?"[12] It suggests that states are like individuals in the state of nature: they preexist legal constraint and are radically free, possessed of free will to (among other things) accept or reject legal obligations.[13]

In the *Nuclear Weapons* opinion, Judge Gilbert Guillaume wrote a dissent that followed in the spirit of *Lotus* and put the legal vacuum theory to work. Having found no evidence that governments have used their free will to construct limits on nuclear weapons, he concluded that the Court had therefore no basis for finding them to be illegal. As Guillaume asserted, "If the law is silent in this case, States remain free to act as they intend."[14] As the ICJ noted in an earlier case, in a legal vacuum the decisions of governments are "inspired by considerations of convenience or of simple political expediency" rather than law, drawing an explicit line between "political" decision making when no law exists and the opposite "legal" decision making after legalization.[15]

The majority in the *Nuclear Weapons* judgment, however, did not follow Guillaume in his reference back to the logic of *Lotus*. Instead, after agreeing with him that there are no explicit legal resources on nuclear weapons, the majority continued to search for ways that state behavior might be connected with legal obligations. This produced two sets of resources that the judges said provided a legal context for framing the issue. First, it said that existing rules on the conduct of war should apply to nuclear weapons, including rules regarding proportionality, distinction, and necessity in armed conflict. This is a fairly conventional reading of the laws of armed conflict, which sees it defining who can be targeted and as indifferent to the kind of weapon being used. It infers rules from existing technologies to the new setting. Second, and more radically, the majority acknowledged that the peculiar destructive capacity of nuclear weapons, what it called the "certain unique characteristics of nuclear weapons," had implications for their lawfulness. But contrary to the hopes of the antinuclear activists who requested the opinion in the first place, the majority used the apocalyptic physical properties of nuclear weapons to find that they could *not* be inherently illegal, and the opinion concluded as a permissive authorization through law of nuclear weapons.

Their logic went as follows: the incredible destructive potential of nuclear weapons technology meant that they should only be used in the extreme case where the very existence of a state was threatened; in the face of such a threat, no other tool of war would be useful to guarantee the survival of the state; for a state in that situation is to survive, it may need to use nuclear weapons; if they are illegal, then this is tantamount to a death sentence for the law-abiding state; this, the majority said, was an unacceptable conclusion, both as a policy outcome and legal finding. The judges inferred from this that it was therefore inconceivable that the governments of the world intended to make nuclear weapons illegal. The priority for national self-preservation made it impossible that weapons of last resort could be inherently unlawful. But failing to find a positive affirmation of their legality, the majority in the end said "it cannot reach a definitive conclusion as to the legality or illegality of the use of nuclear weapons by a State in an extreme circumstance of self-defense in which its very survival is at stake."[16] With this reasoning, the majority replaced the *Lotus* logic advanced by Judge Guillaume with the argument that what extreme self-defense requires must be lawful. And along the way, it erased any possibility that nuclear weapons exist in an unregulated, pre-legal space of unlimited state freedom.

This conclusion is striking both for the way it links state interests and self-defense in determining international legality, and for the permissive substantive outcome that endorses nuclear weapons use as an appropriate response for a government faced with an intense threat to its security. On the first, it echoes Isabel Hull's account of earlier weapons systems; in the pre–World War I era, she documents a similar relationship between German legal justifications and the invention of new weapons, what she calls "weapons positivism." This presumes that the ultimate goal of international law is the preservation of actually existing states and therefore judges the legality of new policy possibilities based on their contribution to that goal.[17] Interpretations of law that impede this goal are rejected as logical contradictions of the idea of international law itself. In the *Nuclear Weapons* opinion, the utility of the weapons in defense of the state makes them lawful, or at least not unlawful. The perceived security needs of the state helps specify the content of international law. This extends the analysis of chapter 4 on the expansive, empowering capacity of legalized self-defense.

The disjuncture between Guillaume and the majority reveals competing conceptions of legality in the absence of law. For Guillaume, the absence of law indicates a gap in legal coverage that then permits the inherent autonomy of states to be expressed. He finds the frontier of international legalization and beyond it sees unfettered free will. New policy possibilities, opened up by new technologies, may exist beyond that edge and are conclusively lawful for states until constrained by new positive law. For the majority, by contrast, even before law can be written around a new technology, it is already governed by legal considerations imported from elsewhere, either from other bodies of law or the presumed ultimate purpose of international law to preserve state security. The majority completed the incompleteness identified by Guillaume, and did it by giving a controlling position to national interests: the new practice is lawful if it is the only way for the state to defend its most important interests.

Though traveling along different routes, both Guillaume and the majority end up at the same substantive conclusion that the use of nuclear weapons is not illegal, though rules on the protection of civilians and so on still apply. Guillaume gets to this point by finding no resources that outlaw the weapons and then applying the principle that the absence of law must mean the absence of any prohibition. The majority gets there by believing that a finding of illegality would make it impossible for a state in emergency to defend its national security and that the law cannot be interpreted in such a way that it puts the state in such danger—thus, the needs of state security establish the legality of the act.

Law and No Law: Drones

The arrival of armed drones as a ready instrument of cross-border killing has presented governments and observers with another instance where they must determine the legality of a practice for which no law has yet been written. In the absence of such law, what goes into figuring out whether targeted killing by drones is legal or not? I am interested here in pilotless drones equipped with explosives and sent to kill people across borders. This is today mostly a US practice and the arguments I examine are mostly anchored in US foreign and military policies.

As with nuclear weapons before them, it is not self-evident which, if any, legal rules apply or how they should be applied to this new weapon. Debates about the legality of the US drones program dive deep into the toolbox of international legal interpretation. There are no treaties or other instruments that directly regulate drones, and therefore no legal obligations specifically attached to them.[18] Their novelty means there cannot plausibly be any customary law around them, although their purpose fits clearly in a long tradition of laws on war. The drones case also lacks a crucial legal document such as the *Nuclear Weapons* opinion provides. It might then be seen as sitting in a lacuna of legalization that represents precisely the kind of prelegalized condition that could be a useful contrast to the postlegalized alternative.

Despite that, neither governments nor activists typically present drones as falling into a policy space that is *beyond* international law, either in the sense of the *Lotus* logic of a legal vacuum or a national security, political question that does not touch on legal issues. To be sure, many observers seem to feel that this is the underlying position of the US government in practice. But in fact almost all the public discussion of drones, for and against, takes for granted the premise that the legality is materially relevant to the policy itself and that it can be ascertained with the right tools of interpretation.[19] The ideology of the rule of law, described in chapter 3, is present throughout.

The drones debate is thoroughly legalized in the sense that the policy is framed by both critics and proponents as a question of what law allows or forbids. It is also clear that state interests play a central role in determining what the law is on drones. In the end, the formal legal debate hinges on whether one believes that the United States is in a legal state of war with its targets, and war depends on self-referential claims about perceived threats to national security. Legality in drones therefore turns on whether they are being used in ways that the United States deems essential for its defense; as with nuclear weapons, legality ends up derivative of state security.

The argument in favor of the legality of US practices, made by US government officials as well as legal and political analysts of various kinds, generally involves two components, though the parts are often mixed together or implied.[20] First, it is said that the United States is in a state of armed conflict with certain enemies and this condition makes it legal to target those people. Second, they suggest that the laws on war do not discriminate among types of weapons, so the differences between drones and (among other things) the piloted bombers of World War II are immaterial to the question. Together, these become the international legal defense for cross-border targeted killing. The United States understands the enemy to be "Al Qaeda, as well as the Taliban and associated forces," and the battlefield to be wherever those people are, whether Pakistan, Afghanistan, Yemen, or anywhere else.[21] Echoing the *Nuclear Weapons* opinion, the United States argues that there is nothing about drones as instruments of war that differentiates them from other weapons for the purposes of international law. In a speech that laid out the Obama administration's legal rationale for drones, Koh said, "The rules that govern targeting do not turn on the type of weapon system used, and there is no prohibition under the laws of war on the use of technologically advanced weapon systems in armed conflict . . . so long as they are employed in conformity with applicable laws of war."[22] The longstanding rules about distinguishing between civilians and combatants, and using force only as a last resort and in a degree that is proportionate to the military advantage being sought, apply to drones as they do to all other instruments. In this view, the distinguishing features of drones—their pilotlessness and precision—raise no legal issues that were not already present in older military practices, including bombing by B-52s, targeting commanders on the battlefield, and more.

The critics of drones address both of these claims. They suggest that the legal frame of armed conflict in the sense developed since the early twentieth century does not apply in this conflict and that the technological features of drones (distance, automation, and low cost) make them more likely than other weapons to facilitate illegal forms of killing.[23] I deal with the second of these first because it helps underscore the centrality of the first question.

It is often said that drones' ability to kill individual targets faraway and at relatively low cost may encourage governments to do this much more frequently than in the past.[24] The opportunity for mistakes are therefore greatly increased, either by misidentifying the person who is targeted, killing innocent bystanders, or intentionally targeting people for reasons that are not grounded in the specific armed conflict that authorized the killing.[25] It also may cause governments to prioritize killing over capturing their enemies, and thus violate both the law-of-war requirement that capture be preferred to killing and rules of due process that obtain outside a battlefield.[26] Critics often claim that the particular features of these weapons make them more likely than others to be used in ways that are illegal. Christoph Heyns, in his role as UN special rapporteur on extrajudicial, summary, or arbitrary executions, emphasized that drone use must accord with existing international legal obligation on individual human rights, especially with the right to life, "widely regarded as the supreme right," which is enshrined in numerous international treaties as well as customary law and many domestic constitutions, and is nonderogable in international law.[27] Amnesty International came to a similar conclusion in a 2013 report that observed that "international law permits the use of lethal force in very restricted conditions . . . [but] from the little information made available to the public, U.S. drone strike policy appears to allow extrajudicial executions in violation of the right to life, virtually anywhere in the world."[28] It concluded that "the [US] administration is killing people outside the bounds of human rights and the law," and followed with the advice that the United States change its practices and bring it into line with existing rules of international law.

These are complaints about how the weapon is used in practice. As such, they set up a debate around whether or not actual US policies are consistent with US legal obligations as they currently exist. The US government responds to them with reassurances that it only uses drones under the most careful criteria, with high standards for information, protection of nontargeted people, and all the requirements of the laws of armed conflict.[29] As Amnesty International notes above, it is difficult to get the empirical evidence needed from either the strike location or US government by which these claims might be verified or challenged—but the debate at this point turns into an empirical one: Does the United States in practice follow the rules or not? It takes existing rules as given and compares US practice to them.

But the empirical questions rest on a deeper disagreement over *which* rules apply: the rules on human rights or the rules of war? The latter are more permissive for government killing and the former more constraining, and so it is not surprising that the US government has sought to fill the apparent legal vacuum with the latter. By advancing different legal frames, the two sides construct alternative legal realities by which US practices should be gauged and use them to advance competing conclusions about their legitimacy. At the heart of the controversy is the existence of an armed conflict between it and the people it targets. In a legal sense, everything hinges on this question.

The presence of war as a legal condition is the switch that determines whether the killing is acceptable, and the laws of war provide the permissive legal environment that the government seeks in order to kill its opponents.[30] As Charlie Savage says, "If the war model is wrong, then a host of wartime measures based on individuals' presumed membership in al-Qaeda—like detaining suspected adversaries indefinitely and killing them in situations where they do not present an imminent threat—are illegal."[31] If the United States is at war, then its targeted killing is lawful as long as it obeys the *jus in bello* laws of armed conflict. If not, then it is unlawful.

The existence of war or armed conflict as a legal condition is not easy to determine. It is at once a factual and legal matter: it depends on how one interprets international legal resources and how one understands what is going on in the real world. Legal reasoning alone will not resolve the debates that ensue, and the ambiguity is productive for agents who seek legitimation through law. Classical public international law from the early twentieth century offers a highly formalist way to identify war, in the shape of an explicit declaration between two states. This is how it was envisioned in the 1909 Hague Convention on the Opening of Hostilities, which made it a legal requirement that "hostilities between [states] must not commence without previous and explicit warning, in the form either of declaration of war, giving reasons, or of an ultimatum with conditional declaration of war."[32] While this retains a place in the popular imagination, the practice of formally declaring war mostly disappeared from state practice after the mid-twentieth century. At the other end of the formalism spectrum, the Geneva Conventions treat war (and the broader category of armed conflict) as a purely empirical phenomenon: war exists if there is armed conflict of some intensity between organized groups.[33] When this exists, the rules of the Geneva Conventions apply to the parties. This approach is both capacious and vague. That serves the purposes of applying international humanitarian law to the widest range of behaviors, which is the goal of the International Committee of the Red Cross which monitors the Geneva Conventions. But it also means its outer limits are impossible to identify and so may make the category less useful in other ways.

The United States advances a view that navigates between the formalism of declared war and empiricism of the International Committee of the Red Cross. Its pursuit of targets via drones today is, it says, continuous with its military response to the 9/11 events, and hence has the legal quality of an armed conflict between the United States and the organizers and supporters of those attacks.[34] It makes this case with a combination of domestic and international legal reasoning. The Congressional Authorization to Use Military Force in 2001 gave the president the authority to "use all necessary and appropriate force against those nations, organizations, or persons he determines planned, authorized, committed, or aided the terrorist attacks that occurred on September 11, 2001, or harbored such organizations or persons, in order to prevent any future such acts of international terrorism against the United States by such nations, organizations, or persons."[35] This is paired with the permissive language on self-defense in Article 51 of the UN Charter to form the legal argument that the United States is engaged in post-9/11 armed conflict with "Al Qaeda, the Taliban, and associated forces."[36] When the United States identifies a person in this category who intends harm to the United States, it claims a self-defense right to use military force against them. As self-defense trumps the nonintervention clauses of the Charter, and the legality of killing enemies in war trumps individual due process and human rights, the legal frame gives the United States a legal foundation for targeted killing.[37] Ryan Vogel says that "if the government reasonably concludes that it is involved in an 'armed conflict,' the government may properly utilize law of war methods," including targeted killing.[38] In 2013, the Obama White House summarized its position in these terms: "America's actions are legal. We were attacked on 9/11. Within a week, Congress overwhelmingly authorized the use of force. Under domestic law, and international law, the United States is at war with al Qaeda, the Taliban, and their associated forces. So this is a just war—a war waged proportionally, in last resort, and in self-defense."[39]

Drone critics point out that this argument is capacious enough to justify killing any person anywhere in the world.[40] The only possible unlawful killings are those done where the US government does not believe that the person poses an imminent threat to US security. The limit on the scope of lawful killing is therefore provided by the internal sense of threat that is gauged by the US government itself. Where a threat exists, as perceived by the United States, drones and other weapons are lawful (within *jus in bello*). As with self-defense in chapter 4, the determination of what constitutes an actionable threat to US security lies within the government, with the effect that the determination of legality around drones ends up being internalized within the determination of security needs by the state itself. The legal vacuum around drones is filled by the desires of the same state whose behavior is being assessed for legality.

This is of course contested by many critics, many of whom use the ambiguity of war as a legal category to arrive at an opposite policy position. The two sides complement each other: they both accept a rule of law paradigm for government decisions and see the drones question as inside the legal framework, neither sees a legal vacuum. Both strive to support their preferred policies with legal reasoning and resources. A finding of illegality would increase the political costs of the policy, in inverse proportion to the amount by which a finding of legality helps legitimate it. They clearly wish to legitimize opposing policy choices with the law, but all sides take for granted that acting lawfully is important, either because they value it themselves or they think others will treat them better for it (or both).[41]

In this sense, the drone debate shows the power of international legalization and productivity of legal gaps. It is good evidence against the international legal skeptics who maintain that law has little effect on world politics.[42] The legitimizing capacity of international law is abundantly clear around drones, as is the near-universal commitment to operating within a rule-of-law framework. Being in an armed conflict makes killing lawful. It is a legal category with a permissive effect that facilitates government action.[43] It therefore holds significant power—a productive power that defines who can be killed; indeed, it defines who *deserves* to be killed.[44] The political stakes of legal arguments are clear in this case. It can mean the difference between life and death.

Implications for Legal Gaps, State Interests, and the Horror Vacui

The cases of nuclear weapons and drones show several things of interest at the intersection of international law and international politics. First of all, it is clear that all sides in these debates attach a great deal of significance to being on the right side of international law. Lawfulness is taken as a crucial attribute of state policy and important criteria for assessing the quality of the state itself. In the two cases I examined here, however, it is unclear what acting lawfully actually means, since in neither case is there a treaty or other definitive piece of law that clearly spells out the rules that govern these new weapons. Other new weapons might exist in a similar situation, and the frequent calls for new treaties on drones, "killer robots," and cyberattacks reflect implicit concerns about the absence of law.[45]

Where nuclear weapons and drones might be expected to display this vacuum, in practice they do not. Instead, they exhibit what Klabbers has called the horror vacui—the impulse to react against a void by filling it with material, such as in this case legal material. He borrows the idea from physics and art history. Klabbers argues that since treaties will always be incomplete gaps in the coverage of black-letter law is unavoidable. If the system is to function then the agents who operate in it will necessarily make use of resources beyond the bounds of formal law to manage around or through these gaps.[46] The formal system of international law, he says, is sustained by this informal work. This outside material might include evidence of past state practice on the subject, *traveaux preparatoires*, analogies and examples from other legal systems, consequentialist claims, state interests, and more. International legal interpretation fills gaps as if "naturally" with nonlegal or nonformal interpretative material whose relevance isn't established by the standard doctrine of sources of international law. This is the international legal horror vacui at work. The concept describes well the phenomenon on display in both the nuclear weapons and drone debates, where the prelegalization condition turns out to be already constituted and regulated by international law.

If the prelegal condition is structured by legal resources already, then the distinction between pre- and postlegalization has lost its essential core, and it then becomes hard to sustain the conventional liberal account of the transition from a no-law condition to the legalized one. As noted in chapters 2 and 3, liberal theorists of international law often assume that the absence of law indicates disorder, suboptimality, or power politics. These are the features that the process of legalization helps remedy. Characteristic of this group, Goldstein and colleagues define legalization as "the decision in different issue areas to impose international legal constraints on governments."[47] This presumes that the prior condition was one in which states were unconstrained by legal obligations and that international law represents a constraint on their autonomy. It adopts the *Lotus* problematic.

The legal vacuum around new weapons is in part filled in by legal resources inferred from the rules on other weapons, but also in part by ideas about the national interests of states themselves.

In the process of legal interpretation, the security needs of governments are invoked either explicitly (by the ICJ in the nuclear weapons opinion) or implicitly (by the US government to cast killing by drone as armed conflict). These state interests are internalized into international law. At one level, this is not surprising: the international rule of law encourages governments to fill the space with legal arguments and resources that are directed toward the goals they seek. But it also means that the direction of change for international law is likely to be toward the interests of the strongest, most legally active governments. The prescription that all governments should "follow international law," which is at the heart of the international rule of law as an ideology, will therefore naturally advance those substantive goals. I take this up again in chapter 7.

The power of state interests in determining legality also reveals features of legalization that theorists of law have long identified as problematic. Bonnie Honig notes how juridification contributes to a displacement of politics; Veitch suggests it creates zones of "irresponsibility" for powerful actors as a logical counterpart to the responsibilities it also assigns; Judith Shklar points out the political implications of "legalism"—that is, the pervasive ideology that "holds moral conduct to be a matter of [legal] rule following."[48] In different ways, these writers advance the idea of the political productivity of law as an alternative to the common liberal assumption that law serves as a framework for politics, neutral among the substantive disagreements. Honig says the liberal approach "confine[s] politics (conceptually and territorially) to the juridical, administrative, or regulative tasks of stabilizing moral and political subjects, building consensus, maintaining agreements, or consolidating communities and identities."[49] Fuad Zarbiyez says it "attempts to keep the game of interpretation within manageable proportions."[50] Shklar sees the common "isolation of the legal system—the treatment of law as a neutral social entity—[as] itself a refined political ideology, the expression of a preference."[51] To prevail in legal interpretation is empowering for one side or the other. The power politics of international legal interpretations is on display.[52]

Conclusion

What does the rule of law mean when there is no law? The *Lotus* principle gives one answer: that states are naturally and absolutely free in the absence of law. The *Nuclear Weapons* and drone debates provide another: that legal obligations pervade global policy space such that legal vacuums are filled as desired by courts, governments, and activists. The cases here show that the former follows logically from the positivist doctrines of international legal theory but it is the latter that seems most commonly deployed in practice. In theory, drones should exist in a legal vacuum, but in practice they do not. The absence of treaty or customary law is obvious. But law already fills the potential legal void. Even though no formal sources govern the technology, it does not exist in the state-of-nature prelegalization condition imagined by the conventional legalization school. The no-law condition doesn't actually exist around drones. It may not exist around any other state practices.

The legal black hole that one might expect to find around a new technology like drones is in practice immediately erased as governments and others import legal resources from adjacent or analogous practices to explain as well as justify their actions, as they use international law to make sense of their actions to themselves and others. The pervasive desire to legitimate policy by legalizing it means that even novel behaviors are understood in terms of existing legal categories. This may lead to changes in those categories, but more important, it also shows the power of international law to structure even those practices that have yet to be formally encompassed by legal instruments. As Koskenniemi says, noted in chapter 3 above, "The concepts and structures of international law . . . are the conditions of possibility for the existence of something like a sphere of the international."[53]

This points to the inescapability of international law, and argues against seeing politics as the baseline of global affairs to which legalization brings new rationality, order, and structure. This illustrates three themes of significance to this book. First, it shows the political importance of acting legally in foreign policy, even where legality is undefined. Second, it illustrates that the liberal view of law as the natural alternative to the state of nature among countries is untenable on its own terms; in today's world, there is no "prelaw" position for states. And third, it demonstrates that international law is as much enabling and permissive as it is constraining.

6

Torture

LEGITIMATION AND LEGALITY

Justice is a thing that is better to give than to receive.
—SLOAN WILSON, *MAN IN THE GREY FLANNEL SUIT*

The expansion of international legal institutions devoted to individual rights is a remarkable development of the past thirty years. Courts, treaties, legal professionals, and activists have increased dramatically, advancing with a normative discourse about their contribution to human welfare and decent global governance. An industry of scholars and activists promotes compliance with these rules and institutions, and generates insights into the design of human rights instruments, influence of courts, power of socialization and legitimation, role of NGOs in domestic and international legal settings, and more.[1] Compliance with human rights law is often seen as self-evidently desirable on the grounds that following the law will lead to better outcomes for innocent individuals.[2] It is used as a yardstick for measuring the character of governments and the strength of international law more generally.

This chapter considers the political productivity of international human rights law by looking at the relationship between the rules against torture and US torture practices in the 2000s. It takes as its starting point that the meaning of "compliance" with the torture ban is contested rather than settled. I examine the law and politics of torture in order to think more deeply about the connection between law, politics, behavior, and legitimacy. The case is useful because the prohibition on torture is almost universally endorsed but also apparently violated with some frequency, and laws on torture feature centrally in the legal and political justifications offered by both the apparent violators and the apparent defenders of the laws.

I use the case to explore how sharply diverging policies can be defended under a single set of relatively clear international rules. Torture is outlawed, but what is "torture"? The line that separates permitted from forbidden treatment of prisoners empowers governments on one side and disempowers them on the other. It produces the stakes that animate the effort to draw that line in specific instances. The abuse of prisoners is rarely as simple as a powerful state choosing to violate the rules because it feels a compelling interest in doing so. It typically also involves a set of legal justifications for the abuse that force the disagreement onto the terrain of legal interpretation. In this dynamic, the distinction between "rules" and "interests" that often characterizes debates about international law in IR is not very helpful.[3] The two are mutually implicating, and a more nuanced view of the relationship between states, rules, and behavior is needed.

From this exploration, we can see the political power of legal justification. Even strong governments that presumably have the capacity to simply go ahead with the policies that they desire appear to value the legitimation that comes from legality. The United States preferred to situate its torture practices within the framework of the international rule of law and specifically the antitorture treaties, at least after their attempt at secrecy failed. This opens up international human rights law and practice with an eye toward the productive power of law, which allows a view into the connections between international legalization and international politics.

It broadens the view to include law's constitutive effects along with the political impact of legalization in situations where compliance is undefined or essentially contested. The controversy over US torture in the 2000s provides an opportunity to examine the productive dynamics among legalization, rule breaking, and rule following that are central to the themes of this book.

It also helps IR scholars to think more clearly about the concept of "legitimacy" as an explanatory variable for global governance and international rule following. Activism around legalized human rights often posits that better legitimation of human rights rules, courts, and institutions is a step toward better compliance with them by governments, which in turn is a step toward the realization of the substantive goal of respect for human rights. This logical sequence interposes legitimacy as an intervening variable between law and compliance, and leads directly to an activist project to increase legitimacy and design processes that are legitimate.[4] This is in line with a long tradition in law and sociology that connects legitimacy with rule compliance.[5]

But the evidence in this chapter undermines the assumption that greater legitimacy leads to greater compliance. The US leaders who authorized torture after 9/11 seemed committed to the ban on torture just as much as they were committed to ensuring that their policies were not outlawed by it. They affirmed and defended the legal prohibition of torture and organized their actions in its light—even while they endorsed in practice a policy that apparently violated it. Both the Bush administration figures who endorsed torture and their critics sought to situate their policy preferences within the ban on torture inside the broader framework of the international rule of law.

The controversy, of course, was located in competing claims of what constituted torture, who was protected, and who was responsible. Both sides used the law against torture to legitimize their actions and support their preferred policies. The fight for international legal interpretation was a proxy for fights over the behavior itself, with legal arguments serving obvious political goals.[6] This is not unusual, as many uses of international law have this shape. My goal in this chapter is not to resolve the legal controversies of US torture; those are explained well elsewhere.[7] Instead, I use the case to explore the connections between legalization and political legitimation that are revealed by the competing uses of international law, and draw implications for thinking about the relationship between international law in international politics more generally.

US torture complicates the conventional assumption that weak compliance is a product of low legitimation of the rules. The antitorture rules are widely seen as legitimate; in the standard view, this would suggest more faithful compliance. But the effect on the Bush administration appears to have been to increase the utility of a legal argument in order to advance the policies they sought. In other words, the fact that the rules were widely seen as legitimate and important made them more useful in the US efforts to defend its behavior. The United States sought to legalize its state torture practices by positioning them in relation to the antitorture legal regime, and deployed the legal regime to defend it, borrowing from the legitimacy of the rules. Widespread support for the rules in their audience was essential to this program of political legitimation through law. This failed of course, but the effort is as much a part of the practice of the international rule of law as are more successful legal-political campaigns.

It is too simple to assume that increasing the legitimacy of an international rule leads to an increase in compliance.[8] To the contrary, the legitimacy of rules constitutes them as resources that can be used by states and other actors in various ways. The productive power of international law is evident in the constitution of torture as a forbidden practice—but this merely sets the structure for the interaction; it does not determine how particular acts will be classified. It creates an incentive to operate within the rules, yet this can be done in many ways—only some of which look like compliance.[9] The link between legitimacy and compliance runs through the complex politics of legal justification and interpretation, where contestation over the meaning of its various terms and structures is potentially empowering for agents.

I divide the chapter into three sections. The first examines the content of the legal regime against torture and its relevance to US behavior in the 2000s. This is largely contained in the CAT and the Geneva Convention of 1949.[10] I make the case that these rules have had a high level of legitimacy in the international community, including in the US government at the time. Given the unmeasurable nature of legitimacy, this case can only be tentative but it is more plausible than any alternative.

The second section then discusses US behavior toward these rules in the years after 9/11 and emphasizes the effort to fit the practice of torture within legal rules that aim to forbid it. The legal arguments they provided are elements in a politics of legitimation that rests on a mix of legitimation and instrumentalism; it requires that socialization to certain norms exists alongside a capacity for agency and strategic manipulation. This is a challenge to conceptions of legitimacy that imagine legitimacy leading naturally to compliance, and for models of international politics that see socialization and strategic action as distinct modes of thought.

The third section outlines implications for the philosophy of international law, and draws links between international law and public diplomacy. Diplomacy is the presentation of public justifications for state policy, and these today are largely made in the language of international law and legality. The ubiquitous practice of legal justification by states shows the mix of constraint and empowerment that is characteristic of legalization in international politics: states must justify their policies in terms of existing international law (constraint) and doing so adds support to those acts (empowerment). The categories and resources with which these justifications are made are constituted by legal texts, past practice, and ongoing interpretation.

Contested claims about compliance are endemic to international law, as they are to all law. Whether over the antitorture regime, use of drones, or laws on war, arguments about compliance are inescapable. These controversies will not be resolved by closer attention to the formal texts of international law. The controversies reflect the political uses of law and thus political utility—and power—of international law. The international rule of law in world politics encompasses these controversies rather than being undermined by them.

Torture in International Humanitarian Law

There is no doubt that torture is prohibited by international law. The universe of international human rights law and norms contains many prohibitions on torture across all classical sources of international law, from treaties to customary law to *jus cogens*, with the effect that no state exists in a legal condition in which torture is not illegal.[11] The specific content of the prohibition is constituted by the particular terms and application of these rules, and so their effect on domestic and international politics depends on what they say, how they have been interpreted, and how they have been put to use.

The Universal Declaration of Human Rights includes the clear statement that "no one shall be subjected to torture or to cruel, inhuman or degrading treatment or punishment" (Art. 5). This was repeated in the International Covenant on Civil and Political Rights and the American Convention on Human Rights of 1969.[12] These are specific incarnations of the more general statement in the UN Charter that its member states "reaffirm faith in fundamental human rights."[13] These treaties, however, do not frame their subject in terms of specific legal obligations binding on signatories, and so they are not of a type that can be complied with or violated; they describe what they say are the aspirations of the signatories or international community.

The key documents for contemporary legal debates are the Convention against Torture (CAT), adopted in 1984 after negotiations in the UN General Assembly, and the Geneva Conventions of 1949, particularly Article 3 on the treatment of people in noninternational conflicts. The CAT defines torture as "any act by which severe pain or suffering, whether physical or mental, is intentionally inflicted on a person for such purposes as obtaining from him . . . information or a confession, punishing him . . . , or intimidating or coercing him . . . , when such pain or suffering is inflicted by or at the instigation of . . . a public official or other person acting in an official capacity" (Art. 1). It requires that a signatory state "take effective legislative, administrative, judicial or other measures to prevent acts of torture in any territory under its jurisdiction" (Art. 2), and "ensure that all acts of torture are offenses under its criminal law" (Art. 4).

The Geneva Conventions of 1949 prohibit "violence to life and person, in particular murder of all kinds, mutilation, cruel treatment and torture" (3rd, 3[i]a), and "outrages upon personal dignity, in particular, humiliating and degrading treatment" (3rd, 3[i] c). These apply in cases of declared war among contracting parties (Art. 2) as well as conflicts of a noninternational character (Art. 3). This is the set of treaties that includes the three earlier Geneva Conventions (of 1864, 1906, and 1929) and adds a fourth, and has been ratified by every member of the United Nations; this makes it the centerpiece of international human rights law as it applies to behavior in the context of war and other armed conflict. The CAT goes further, making it clear that "no exceptional circumstance whatsoever, whether a state of war or a threat of war, internal political instability or any other public emergency, may be invoked as a justification of torture" (Art. 2[2]).

Both the CAT and the Geneva Conventions are interstate treaties, which means that the obligations that each contains are binding only on the states that accept them. They do not directly apply to individuals, even though individual persons undertake the acts that the treaties aim to suppress.[14] This creates an interesting opening between law and responsibility. Public international law has traditionally been understood as having only states as its subjects and does not regulate the conduct of individual persons (though pirates may be seen as holding special status under international law). There is therefore a gap between the prohibition of torture as a matter of interstate law and the legal position of the individuals whose conduct is presumably ultimately of interest to the law. To get from a public international law commitment against torture to an obligation that is binding on individuals, whether private actors or public officials, requires some kind of bridge from international law to either domestic or international criminal law.

For the CAT, its Article 4 provides the bridge. The article requires that torture be made a criminal offense in the domestic law of its signatory states. As such, it exploits existing domestic legal regimes in order to create a workable legal obligation that impinges on the torturer as an individual as opposed to on the state. For the Geneva Conventions, the gap is bridged by Article 1, which is common across all four of the conventions, and reads, "The High Contracting Parties undertake to respect and to ensure respect for the present Convention in all circumstances." This must be done with domestic legislation and military codes of conduct binding on the states' military personnel.

The operation of this domestic implication was explained for the CAT in the 2012 decision *Belgium v. Senegal* at the ICJ.[15] The Court decided that Senegal committed a harm to Belgium by not prosecuting Hissène Habré for crimes covered under the torture convention. Habré, the former president of Chad, had been living in Senegal for several years despite evidence of his responsibility for torture while in office. The ICJ reached several interesting conclusions in its decision: first, on jurisdiction, it found that the disagreement between Belgium and Senegal over how the CAT should be implemented was indeed a "legal dispute" and thus the Court's jurisdiction was activated; second, on substance, it found that Senegal's failure to act against Habré amounted to a violation of its promises to other signatory states; and finally, it found that Belgium, as one of these states, had its international legal rights harmed by that violation and so was in a position to bring the matter to the ICJ as a contentious case. The Court demanded that Senegal use its domestic criminal institutions to prosecute Habré for torture. Should Senegal fail in that obligation, it said, it must instead extradite him to a state where he would be prosecuted under domestic law.[16] The case shows the path by which the international obligation taken on by the government in signing the CAT is executed through changes in domestic criminal law and also how this remains at the same time an international obligation over which the ICJ exercises oversight authority.

Other international human rights instruments can be compared on how they do or do not deal with reaching individuals. The Genocide Convention, for instance, includes an obligation for domestic legal internalization much like the CAT. It requires that its states' parties "enact, in accordance with their respective Constitutions, the necessary legislation to give effect to the provisions" of the convention that criminalize genocide as well as set the terms for investigating and punishing those who commit it (Art. 5). This puts the crime of genocide into the domestic criminal codes of all signatory states. The Rome Statute of the International Criminal Court is revolutionary because it bridges the gap by creating an entirely new international institution and giving it "jurisdiction over natural persons."[17] It also includes the commitment by states parties to accept that their citizens (as well as foreigners within their jurisdictions) may be prosecuted by the International Criminal Court directly under certain conditions. This may amount to a new move by public international law toward seeing the individual person as the subject rather than a state, though it can equally be seen as a state-centric act of delegation to an international institution.[18]

There are other international human rights instruments that make no effort to bridge between states' obligations to each other and the legal standing of individuals. For instance, there is nothing in the UN Charter, International Covenant on Civil and Political Rights, or Universal Declaration of Human Rights that requires that individuals refrain from, or be punished for, acts of torture; in each of these instruments, the commitment against torture is made as a promise (or aspiration) by states to other states.

In the United States, the bridge between international law on torture and domestic law is accomplished in several ways. The War

Crimes Act of 1996 makes grave breaches of the Geneva Conventions into federal crimes. In the domain of torture more broadly, the formal language of torture is used in US criminal law only to refer to acts committed abroad, while much of the substantive behavior that the CAT is concerned with within the United States falls under the Eighth Amendment to the US Constitution. The Criminal Code defines torture as "an act committed by a person under the color of law specifically intended to inflict severe pain and suffering" (18 U.S. Code §2340), when the act was committed abroad. Inside the United States, these acts fall under the constitutional prohibition on "cruel and unusual punishments." The same acts committed by private actors without any connection to the purposes of the state (that is, without "color of law" or "an official capacity") would be covered by criminal laws against assault, murder, and so on. Police brutality in Chicago, for instance, cannot be prosecuted as torture strictly speaking, since it is domestic to the United States.[19]

The international antitorture regime represents an archetypal piece of public international law in the sense that it comes from explicit black-letter treaties that have effect as a result of state consent. It is relatively clear as treaty law goes, and sets out what Andrea Liese considers to be a "non-derogable and absolute" prohibition.[20] They are designed to change the costs and benefits that governments face as they consider how they treat individuals in their custody, and specifically to increase the political costs of using torture. Their behavioral mechanism is to induce compliance by government authorities, and hence they fit into a traditional frame in the legal architecture in world politics. This is consistent with conventional accounts of the philosophy of international law and international rule of law as set out in chapter 2, and with a "compliance model" of law in IR.

The rules are also clearly designed for a nonideal world; the CAT treaty anticipates that violations will occur and sets rules about states' responses to instances of torture. Most of its articles deal with the obligations of states when acts of torture are committed either by their officials or against their citizens. These are rules that are grounded in the practical realities of interstate relations.

Legitimacy

The legitimacy of these rules also seems well established. While I accept that it is impossible to conclusively measure legitimacy in international society, several streams of evidence suggest that states and activists see these rules as highly legitimate. They are among the most widely ratified human rights instruments—the Geneva Convention by 194 jurisdictions and the CAT by 147. They are endorsed even by groups that are not qualified to ratify them such as rebel militias and other groups that actively seek out affiliation with the rules, presumably looking for some political legitimacy that they believe is attached to them.[21] There is little dissent from the idea that the rules are binding on the states that have accepted them, and that they are both normatively and legally good; that is, they are accepted as important legal commitments by states and are endorsed as reflecting normative progress in world politics.[22] For instance, Louise Arbour, the UN high commissioner for human rights, was likely speaking for the majority opinion when she said that the "absolute ban on torture . . . [is] a cornerstone of the international human rights edifice."[23] When controversies arise over torture in international law, it almost without fail centers on the question of how to make governments follow the rules more faithfully. It is never about whether the rules should exist or not. There is essentially no controversy over the rules, and no mobilization to abolish or limit them; all discussion is about their implementation, extension, or enforcement. The absence of controversy is unlikely to be "artificial" in the sense of being either a result of either the exclusion of dissent by the imposition of political power or fundamental irrelevance of the rules.

Perhaps most telling among the evidence for the legitimation of antitorture laws is the fact that even those who argue in favor

of "coercive interrogation" or "exceptional measures" work hard
to maintain the illegality of torture.[24] Michael Ignatieff represents
this position, suggesting that torture should be outlawed *and* (not
but) the government should be allowed to use coercive interrogation measures in certain circumstances, with special bureaucratic
or political approval.[25] A different route to the same outcome is
taken by Alan Dershowitz with "torture warrants"; he suggests
that torture is rightly outlawed in international law, *but* since it
continues to be practiced by states, it should be used only according to certain bureaucratic or political procedures (that is, warrants to permit torture must be obtained first) so that the practice
is accompanied by greater accountability.[26] They maintain their
support for the ban on torture, but Ignatieff would allow coercive
interrogation while Dershowitz would allow violations of the law
when authorized by the state.

The conventional understanding of legitimacy in social science
suggests that a well-legitimated rule or process should produce
higher rates of compliance by its target audience. Legitimation is
said to create an internal motivation toward rule following, and
legitimation is therefore often sought as a mechanism for increasing compliance and reducing opposition.[27] This connection between compliance and legitimacy is evident across the spectrum
of scholarship, and originates in the sociological literature from
which the IR literature is derived; it is present in Max Weber's view
of legitimacy, Jürgen Habermas's model of communicative action,
John Gaventa's theory of acquiescence and social power, consent
theory, democratic theory, and beyond.

The legitimacy literature in IR contains two streams that arrive
at this conclusion by distinct paths, reflecting competing visions
of how to study legitimacy in social settings. A *subjective tradition*
defines legitimacy as the belief by an individual that a rule or structure has rightful authority. This traces back to Weber's sociological
theory of legitimacy, in a "descriptive" rather than "normative"
attitude. It begins from the premise that legitimacy rests on the
ideas held by an actor about their social surroundings. These ideas

may be shared among many in a community, but are reducible to an individual belief: because individuals behave differently toward rules that they believe are legitimate, the existence of a belief about legitimate rule has consequences for aggregate social and political systems.[28] In contrast to this, an *objective tradition* on legitimacy begins by asking what kinds of rules or structures are deserving of these beliefs, and posits external normative criteria, often derived from moral philosophy, to judge whether a rule or institution can be called legitimate. Common among these criteria are versions of democratic procedures or substantive goals, such as fairness or respect for human rights. This view suggests that outside observers can judge the legitimacy of a rule by observing its content, genealogy, or relationship to the governed.[29]

The subjective tradition has an affinity with behavioral studies in social science, and focuses on how people (or states) behave in the face of political authorities that they believe to be legitimate (or illegitimate). The objective tradition has more in common with normative philosophy, and has the power to second-guess people's own beliefs about the legitimacy of the institutions around them. For instance, Tom Tyler, following the subjective tradition, investigates when and why people in the United States obey laws and decisions that do not favor them.[30] He finds that people are more likely to follow the law when they believe that the process that produced it is legitimate. He does not ask whether these beliefs are justified. By contrast, Allen Buchanan suggests that a government should only be considered legitimate when it meets certain standards for the treatment of its citizens, regardless of how the population feels about it.[31] This is characteristic of the objective approach: Buchanan posits a set of morally valuable criteria and then uses them to judge whether a government should count as legitimate.

The traditions coexist because each can illuminate the blind spots of the other. On the one hand, the objective approach is only as compelling as the moral criteria that it begins with, and these are endlessly contested in political philosophy. The subjective approach, on the other hand, takes seriously people's beliefs about their political surroundings but provides no critical resources for assessing those beliefs; political leaders routinely try to legitimize their rule to their subjects and may succeed even if outsiders find the regime abhorrent. The two approaches therefore mean different things when they conclude that a rule or institution is legitimate. These differences often keep the sides from talking clearly with each other.

The two traditions agree, however, that legitimacy produces compliance. The objective tradition suggests that agents have a moral or political reason to comply with legitimate rules (a "duty to obey"), while the subjective tradition finds empirical evidence that they in fact do comply with them more than rules without legitimacy. Conversely, rule violation is in this view both evidence of the absence of legitimacy and a delegitimating force. Rules and institutions, it is said, lose their legitimacy and thus their power if they are routinely violated, just as law loses its bindingness through desuetude. As Johan Karlsson Schaffer, Andreas Føllesdal, and Geir Ulfstein note, "If a treaty . . . fails to secure its objective to a certain minimum extent, it risks losing normative legitimacy; individuals and other actors may no longer regard themselves as bound to comply."[32] Thus, increasing the legitimacy of a rule is said to increase the likelihood that it will be respected in the policy choices of states, which motivates the search for strategies of legitimation that might cause this to happen.

The politics around the international laws on torture do not fit this model. The rules apparently have a high degree of legitimacy in both the objective and subjective senses, and yet their near-universal acceptance by states as rules that represent the "good" has obviously not produced commensurate compliance. Many signatories of the treaties described above have used torture, apparently in violation of their commitments. Torture remains an option that is used with some frequency by governments and their agents. It can be found in almost all settings of political power; it appears in the practice of all kinds of regimes, including democracies and dictatorships, and is used in the pursuit of all kinds of political objectives, foreign policy, domestic policy, and other aims.[33]

My interest here is in how the apparent rule breaking relates to the apparent legitimacy of the rules. The fact of the continuing and extensive practice of torture despite the antitorture legal regime might be interpreted as evidence that the rules are in fact not seen as legitimate, the rules are not consequential, or legitimation and compliance are distinct concepts without a natural affinity. I pursue the third possibility by suggesting that international rules such as those on torture do gain power by being widely seen as legitimate, but that this power is not manifest by an increase in compliance, at least not as compliance is conventionally understood. Legitimacy constitutes the rules as salient and useful resources for defining the practice, and these rules are the discursive material with which agents fight over political legitimation. Noncompliance of a type can coexist with legitimated rules without undermining either the rules or the concept of legitimacy. The key is to take a more sophisticated approach to the relationship between agents and structures in social settings.

The Legal Framework for US Torture

The tension between rule and practice in this case is notable for many reasons. Most obviously, the failure to forgo torture is a compelling humanitarian catastrophe for the victims, and perhaps a political and legal disaster for the perpetrators.[34] It also points to important questions about the weakness of international treaties and enforcement. For this chapter, I am interested in the relationship that it reveals between law, power, and noncompliance: What does it mean for the politics of legitimation that a rule so apparently well legitimated is also violated at a nontrivial rate?

The US government under George W. Bush consistently maintained its claim to compliance with international law on torture. Bush famously said in 2005, "We do not torture." By way of explanation, he suggested that "there's an enemy that lurks and plots and plans to hurt America again. And so, you bet we will aggressively pursue them. But we will do so under the law."[35] President Donald Trump similarly said, "I want to do everything within the bound of what you're allowed to do legally."[36] This reflects both the power of legality in world affairs and the common perception in the US government that what international law allows is naturally aligned with US foreign policy interests. Similar claims to inherent rule following are evident in other areas of US international policy, including the legality of killing Osama bin Laden, ban on aggressive war, and use of robots in war.[37] In all these cases, the state appears certain of the legality of its behavior, and provides an explanation for how the relevant international rules are coincident with its interests and policies.

The tenure of Bush as president of the United States, especially the first term, is frequently characterized as being indifferent or hostile to the rules of international law, "lawlessness" and an "attack on international law," or the "dramatic rejection of international legal constraints."[38] Many then saw in Barack Obama's presidency a "return" to international law and cooperation, and Donald Trump as its radical repudiation.[39] With respect to torture specifically, the Bush administration enacted policies regarding the interrogation of prisoners in blatant violation of its international legal commitments.[40] It did this in secret at first, but continued the practice under new political and legal justifications once it was exposed to the public.[41] There is little doubt that these actions, and perhaps the policy making that backed them up, constituted grave breaches of the Geneva Convention (assuming the United States was in a condition of war or armed conflict) and violations of the CAT, meaning that those who approved and executed them put themselves in legal jeopardy under the war crimes provisions of the US Criminal Code and other statutes.

Yet it is equally true that the Bush administration invested heavily in justifying its behavior through law. It used the laws on torture as the framing around which it constructed these explanations.[42]

The effort was invested in showing that whatever the US conduct was, it was *not* the thing described in the CAT.[43] These arguments have been widely rejected as legally unsound, but they are significant in the politics of legitimation. The investment made in situating US policy within the law shows that the international legal architecture on human rights was indeed important to the Bush administration. They seemed to feel that as a political matter, a legal justification was useful and perhaps necessary.

As evidence of US torture became public, the United States offered three kinds of legal arguments to substantiate its claim to rule compliance: it said that prisoners in US custody did not qualify for the legal protections of the antitorture regime; the particular practices of US interrogations, including waterboarding, did not satisfy the standard of torture in international and domestic law; and the US Constitution allowed the president to supersede international law in extremis. These arguments used the resources of the international legal regime on torture in order to reconcile US behavior to the rules and ultimately support US justifications for its policies. It represents an appeal to international law in general and reinvestment in the rules prohibiting torture in particular—done in the service of avoiding legal responsibility for rule violation.

The first claim was essentially about jurisdiction and rested on the contention that the individuals that the United States was holding as a result of its "war on terror" were not of the types described as qualifying for protection under any of the Geneva Conventions. This assertion was developed by the now-notorious legal team in the Office of Legal Counsel at the Department of Justice, which in January 2002 wrote advice for the president, who then adopted it in February of that year.[44] The policy said that conflict with al-Qaeda was outside the scope of the Geneva Conventions because it was neither interstate nor noninternational, and so the legal terms in the Third Geneva Convention were not relevant to prisoners captured in that conflict. No US behavior toward the people it held in captivity could violate the rules because these people were not part of the group protected by the rules. With respect to the war in Afghanistan, the United States accepted that this conflict did create antitorture obligations on the United States with regard to prisoners of war, but it claimed that its detainees were not prisoners of war because they were not organized as a militia, with uniforms and command structure, and did not themselves abide by the laws of war.[45] To accommodate both sets of people, the United States created the new category of "illegal enemy combatant" to describe a person who was excluded from protections guaranteed to combatants in interstate war versus those guaranteed to "irregulars" and fighters in noninternational wars. As such, there was no legal requirement, the United States held, to follow any particular course of protection for their rights.

The second claim arose from close readings of the CAT, the US Criminal Code, and other documents that outlaw torture. The argument here was that the behaviors of interest to the United States, including beatings, waterboardings, mock executions, and animal threats, were not encompassed by the term torture in these instruments. The content of torture was instead said to be limited to those acts that produce pain "equivalent in intensity to the pain accompanying serious physical injury, such as organ failure, impairment of bodily functions, or even death," or mental harm that persists for months.[46] At the same time, the United States took the view that to qualify as torture, the torturer had to "have the intent to inflict severe pain or suffering," as opposed to inflicting pain incidental to the intent to acquire information. For US domestic law, Justice Antonin Scalia of the Supreme Court later offered the view that these might not constitute violations of the Eighth Amendment either since they were not primarily intended as "punishments" relevant to that amendment.[47] One by one, the behaviors of interest to the United States were identified and excluded from the legal definition of torture that applied to US personnel. They were then bundled under the heading of "enhanced interrogation techniques" and set outside the bundle of practices that are illegal.

Finally, the administration maintained that under some circumstances, the US president was not bound by the international legal commitments taken on by the United States. The Bybee memo suggested that the president was essentially unregulated by Congress or international law in his commander-in-chief duties such that the treatment of detainees in the so-called war on terror was at his discretion.[48] This also applied, it said, to the behaviors of subordinates to the president who were acting on his instructions. The constitutional position of the president relative to other legal institutions meant that the torture prohibitions were not constraints on his authority or the behavior of his delegated agents.

This generated a great deal of criticism among scholars of US constitutional law and others, as did all the apologist arguments.[49] Each fails in the face of either logic or law, and none has survived as the operative position of the US government. But this does not mean they are unimportant; their deployment in defense of US torture reflects the political importance of international legal justification. Their role in political debates over torture was to open up space within the rule of law where that which was banned by the rules could be practiced without violating them. The US government in this case was committed to remaining within the framework of legalized politics in this sense.

Inside and Outside Legality

The Bush administration did not convince many people that its actions were lawful. But its use of legal arguments did have the effect of framing the controversy as a set of questions about international law and legality. The episode thus both reveals and reinforces the authority of international law over governments. It turned the debate into a matter of international legal interpretation, with the effect of empowering people who have a role in that process as well as giving special status to arguments, resources, and practices of international law. It also disempowered the US government in a way by acknowledging that its authority sits in a subordinate position to international legal rules and forms. It shows the governance authority that is granted to the idea of the international rule of law while maintaining the possibility for strategic, self-centered agency on the part of states within that authority as they attempt to make use of international legal resources to advance their own interests.

Legal arguments about torture resonated in the politics of legitimation. This effect is distinct from the legal persuasiveness of the contentions themselves. It shows why we should not dismiss these arguments as merely self-serving gloss on self-evidently illegal behavior. It is true that the US provided self-serving legal justifications overlaid on rule breaking. The capacity and incentive to this reveals rather than diminishes the political impact of international law. These justifications have important social consequences precisely because they invoke powerful legal resources in the service of political ends.

The US government showed tremendous deference to international law. At the most general level, it accepted that US foreign policy should fit within its legal obligations. This is both an empirical claim—that it *does*—and normative commitment—that it is *right* that it does. These are common refrains in US foreign policy; the idea of the United States as a "rule-of-law nation" is part of its standard narrative.[50] To take just one example, Obama said in his Nobel speech, "Where force is necessary, we have a moral and strategic interest in binding ourselves to certain rules of conduct. . . . [E]ven as we confront a vicious adversary that abides by no rules . . . the United States of America must remain a standard bearer in the conduct of war. That is what makes us different from those whom we fight. That is the source of our strength."[51] Ikenberry has made this into a more general argument about the twentieth century in his suggestion that the post–World War II international order is characterized by its commitment to international rules rather than bare power politics: as a "rules-based system," it represents a progressive change from previous eras.[52] In this case, the United States endorsed the meta-norm of foreign policy and IR that says that the rules of international law should be obeyed.

It also accepted that this applied to the specific practices in question here. The United States made use of the key texts and customs of human rights law, and constituted from them what it presented as a sound interpretation fully embedded in accepted traditions of international legal interpretation. This is evident in the detailed legal defense outlined above as well as the "rendition" programs that sent prisoners to be tortured by other governments instead of by the United States, the choice to locate the prison at Guantanamo Bay, Cuba, with its murky relation to US law, the invention of enhanced interrogation and enemy combatant as means to avoid the categories of torture and prisoner of war, and other measures that situated US conduct at a particular relation to antitorture rules. These choices reveal deference to international law on the part of the United States that accepts the dominance of international law over sovereign states as a form of governance.

For their part, many critics of US conduct agreed with the general framing of the rule of law as the appropriate setting for US foreign policy and were eager to take up the challenge of meeting the US government on the "battlefield" of legal interpretation.[53] Their reading of international law produced an opposite conclusion regarding the lawfulness of the behavior, and their victory in legal and public circles had powerful political effects: the United States abandoned many of its legal arguments, adopted a more encompassing definition of torture, and perhaps even began treating some of its prisoners better.[54]

The juridification of a question has characteristic effects on its politics. As I noted in chapter 3, MacCormick and others have pointed out the "narrowing" that accompanies legalization, as juridical forms demand a specific type of discourse and admit particular kinds of evidence and set aside others. What MacCormick calls "the special sort of [juridical] reasoning" admits certain kinds of arguments and evidence, and refuses others. It "leaves aside any general or abstract deliberation on what in a given context would be best or would all things considered [be] right to do or not do."[55] Kenneth Abbott and Duncan Snidal have said, "Legalization entails a specific discourse, requiring justification and persuasion in terms of applicable rules and pertinent facts."[56] Ingo Venzke agrees: "Legal contestation . . . implies that interpretive claims take a particular argumentative form."[57] In choosing to fight for its policies on the terrain of legality, the United States accepted that the key question should be what the law allowed or forbade. This empowered lawyers and related experts on international law as the key voices in the debate, both within the government and outside.[58] And it meant that legal resources and modes of argument would be decisive. Instead of a debate over political, moral, consequential, or other assessments of torture, it led to debates among lawyers over their close readings of international treaties.

On this terrain, Veitch has noted an important double movement: as law defines what is forbidden, it also defines what is permitted. This is a necessary implication of legalization: the two functions arrive together. The political consequence is that there is permissive power even in a law that aims to forbid something. As we saw in chapter 4, the law against war is permissive of self-defense. Veitch's more general interest is the political concept of responsibility, which comes to be treated as a legal question in contract law and elsewhere. He illustrates his point with reference to landlord-tenant contracts that specify the responsibilities of each party. If something goes wrong in the apartment that is not legally the responsibility of the landlord, then the tenant is expected to bear the costs. Over these matters, the landlord enjoys what Veitch calls a "zone of irresponsibility." Legalization necessarily provides both responsibility and irresponsibility. It "facilitate[s] the dispersals and disavowals of responsibility that together may be seen to constitute the practices of irresponsibility."[59]

The double movement is apparent in the torture case. The laws against torture define the prohibited act in specific legal terms and this opens the door to both condemning those who commit them and a kind of nonresponsibility for those who do not. It reveals a path for the United States or other actors to legitimate their actions by showing them to be outside the set that the law prohibits. This exculpatory capacity is as much a product of the legalization of international politics as is the condemnation that comes from violating the rules. The law gave protorture officials some tools with which to construct a legal space for torture within or alongside the antitorture regime. To the extent that this worked, its effect would be to insulate behavior from legal responsibility. It would reverse the expectation of advocates for the juridification of international human rights.[60]

In this dynamic, the inner motivations of individuals are largely irrelevant. It doesn't matter if the lawyers really "believe" the legal arguments they are making or not, nor does it matter whether they are making them in order to insulate themselves from criminal responsibility, improve the reputation of their government, or for some other reason. Similarly, they may (or may not) have a deeply seated self-image as a rule-following agent, and this doesn't change the basic pattern. My point is this: in the presence of the idea of the international rule of law and specific legal rules and structures on torture, the politics of torture unfold differently than they would without them. Juridification provides a framework and set of resources that shift the terrain of debate from overtly political arguments over what should be done and who is responsible for what harms to "technical" legal arguments about what constitutes compliance.[61]

The torture case shows the power of international legal politics even in the absence of a clear sense of what the rules allow or forbid. It is in that way a corrective to the legal positivism that often shapes studies of international legal politics. In the conventional model set out in chapter 2, the rule of law requires that rules be relatively stable and commonly known. They allow agents to differentiate between lawful and unlawful conduct, and so shape their incentives, and the gap between rule following and rule breaking is clear.[62] This makes it possible for Madeleine Albright, for instance, to distinguish "law-abiding" countries from "rogue states" and "terrorists" on the basis of their behavior toward international law.[63] When seen as a practice instead of a set of rules, the international rule of law appears to be less about compliance with the law and more about the use of law to advance interests. The "problem" of torture will not be resolved by providing ever-clearer definitions in law, enhancing the legitimacy of rule following in general, or socializing states to be "norm followers" as opposed to "interest followers."[64]

Around torture, we see almost universal support for the expressive content of the rules (that is, the ban on torture) but much disagreement on the application of the rules to particular cases. All sides declare themselves supportive of the rule of law as an ideology while legitimating their preferences with competing discourses of legality. In the "postenactment" life of the law, its political uses may well surprise those who wrote it.[65]

This raises the question of what international law is *for* if not for either "making states comply" or "improving human welfare." The standard answer is that it distinguishes rightful from forbidden conduct.[66] It is in this spirit that Bull said that the job of the international lawyer is to "state what the rules of international law are" to their government.[67] This is insufficient when one looks at the effects of international law on state practice.

The role of international law is best described in terms from Koh: "By imposing constraints on government action, law legitimates and gives credibility to government action."[68] This does not depend on a consensus over the line between compliance and noncompliance. As Peter Lindseth has said of EU law, "The very nature of public law has itself deeply evolved. It has become less a system of rules marking seemingly clear lines between 'valid' and 'invalid' exercises of authority, as classical understandings of . . . the rule of law might have demanded. Instead, public law has evolved toward something more focused on 'the allocation of

burdens of reason-giving,' or . . . 'accountability.' "[69] Law legitimates, even if we don't agree on its content.

Conclusion

When the United States was abusing prisoners, it also did two
other things: it claimed that it was not breaking the rules, and it
provided an interpretation of international law with which it
sought to substantiate its claims. This chapter explored the effects of international legalization on the politics of torture in US
foreign policy. Rather than ask whether the United States was
complying with or violating the law, I look instead at how the
laws against torture were used by the United States and its critics
in the political dispute over how US power should be used. Each
side sought to legitimate its policy position by showing it to be
more faithful to international legal texts and traditions. The disagreement over the content of the rules took place in the context
of a shared certainty that state policy should conform to international rules. This mutual commitment to the idea of the international rule of law was the condition of possibility for the dispute
over torture and foreign policy that ensued. It constituted the
terms of the disagreement, created a shared set of resources to
draw from, and gave the contest its stakes—the legitimacy that
comes from acting lawfully and political costs that come from its
opposite.

The juridification of international politics meant that a fight
over the meaning of treaty compliance took the place of a more
overt competition over the use of state power by the United
States.[70] The connections between US torture and international
law run deep. The idea that torture is an international crime is itself
a product of international legalization, as is the definition of what
acts are prohibited and what are allowed. The ideology of the international rule of law invests the former (lawbreaking) with negative political valence and the latter (law following) with positive,

and creates the incentive felt by officials to legitimate their policies through legalization.

The widespread acceptance of the laws against torture by governments may not actually decrease the prevalence of torture in the world. But it does cause debates around torture to be framed by the ban; the law provides the resources with which arguments about torture are made. This is at one level a depressing conclusion, since it means that the strategies of legitimation argued over by activists and scholars may not be reliable devices for improving the situation of those who might become victims in the future. It sustains the view that the laws are indeed powerful, however, even over powerful states and nonaccountable leaders; the need to justify oneself according to the rules makes those leaders dependent on those rules and their self-serving legal arguments about compliance. This dependence makes them vulnerable. Their arguments can be met with counterarguments drawn from the same resources, and the political and legal costs of being seen to lose this argument can be high. Where there exist institutions to organize this accountability, such as the International Criminal Court or national criminal courts willing to claim jurisdiction, the practical life of international rules can be compelling on individuals. This is not impeded by the fact that even well-legitimated rules contain within them the possibility of endless competing interpretations of compliance and noncompliance.

7

The Empire of
International Legalism

Empire is . . . the sovereign power that governs the world.
—MICHAEL HARDT AND ANTONIO NEGRI, *EMPIRE*

What does it mean that "the rules themselves" appear to govern, as Quesnay said to the dauphin in the opening epigraph? Throughout this book, I have shown that the rule of law provides a framework for state behavior at once inescapable, productive, and politically motivated. In this setting, states invoke, manipulate, and evade legal resources, but the rule of law remains supreme. The international system is not anarchic; governments are subordinate to law. Where liberal theorists have been mistaken, though, is in the assumptions that follow from this observation. Liberals argue that as a political structure of authority and governance, law must constrain state action and place states on a more even playing field. Indeed, law does constrain. But it also empowers states—and empowers them unequally—and maintains inequalities in the international system. This is not a defect of law, and recognizing it does not indicate that law is unimportant. Just the opposite. Rule of law constitutes the international system. Its ideological demands condition every policy. States operate within a veritable empire of legalism.

The Rule of Law as a Structure of Governance

At the ideological and philosophical heart of international law is governments' obligation to comply with the rules to which they have agreed. This commitment—endorsed virtually universally by states, activists, and scholars—defines the political relationship between the legal system and state sovereignty. *Pacta sunt servanda*: agreements must be honored. From this premise flows every other belief about international law—how it works, what it does, and what is at stake in following it. Pacta sunt servanda is the basis of an interstate version of what Shklar calls "legalism": the idea that rightful conduct follows from complying with law.[1] Legalism fosters hierarchy because it specifies a clear line of authority from the legal system at the top to subjects below. Governments—subjects, in the international system—may consent to or reject individual pieces of law, but they cannot escape the expectation of adherence to law. "State sovereignty and the rule of law," Ikenberry says, "are part of the deep operating logic" of the global order.[2]

This arrangement is something like a constitution for the international political system. As Besson puts it, "In the context of international law, constitutional discourse is . . . used mainly by reference to the material constraints certain international legal norms place on national but also on regional and international law-making processes."[3] As our case studies have shown, the political commitment of pacta sunt servanda is one of these global norms, constraining—but also enabling—policy making.

The constitutional status of rule following is reflected in the political power of legal justifications. Legal justifications have political power *because* of a shared ideological commitment to rule following. Whether these justifications are genuine or instrumental is less important than that agents act as if it matters to them.

Consider Antje Wiener's incisive observation that "the mode of contestation, that is the way that contestation is displayed in practice, depends on the . . . environment where contestation takes place."[4] In the global political environment today, the mode of contestation is legal. Legitimacy is the prize over which states compete, and it is won and lost through adherence to law—which is to say, skillful deployment of legal resources. This is how we know that the ideology of the rule of law governs global politics. Whether the results are emancipatory and beneficial to human welfare, or whether they justify aggression, repression, and coercion are open questions.

The permissive and constraining effects associated with legalism are two sides of the same coin. All arise from the fact that illegal action is more politically difficult than legal action. Illegal action imposes reputational costs and forces leaders to contend with greater internal resistance—penalties that encourage governments to support their policies with legal arguments and justification. But this is also the source of international law's permissive power. By presenting acts as lawful, governments seek the political legitimation that comes from behaving legally in a rule-of-law setting. The results, as we have seen, include the expansion of wars of self-defense since 1945 and an episode in which the United States practiced torture under the legally inspired heading of enhanced interrogation.

The political arrangement created by the international rule of law contradicts the common view that states exist in anarchy. This was illustrated in the *Kadi* case, as developed by Wiener and colleagues. When the Security Council, using its authority over international security, imposed targeted sanctions on Kadi, he objected that his legal rights to due process had been violated. He was vindicated by the European Court of Justice in a ruling that enforced the priority of the rule of law over the domain of "politics" that is the Council's remit.

International anarchy is conventionally understood as a space or set of relations in which there is no overarching authority. Waltz famously said that in international politics, "each is the equal of all the others. None is entitled to command; none is required to obey."[5] This differentiates the international political structure from domestic, "governed" systems, and always will. It is this condition of anarchy that James Crawford and Martti Koskenniemi have in mind when they say that classical international law "regards each state as sovereign, in the sense that it is presumed to have full authority to act both internally and at the international level."[6]

The anarchy model suggests that the space between states is empty, and states simply do what they can in pursuit of security, balance of power, cooperation, and so forth. States may use international institutions to manage their interdependence across this ungoverned void, but the void is not therefore governed. Scholars of global governance often see international institutions as bridges that span these gaps and make it possible to manage "the world's problems that cannot be limited to national governments."[7]

Yet this apparent void is not in fact empty. Pacta sunt servanda is its organizing principle, which generates the resources, incentives, and politics we have so far discussed. As long as international politics takes place within the structure of authority provided by the rule of law, the system is governed rather than anarchic. In Newtonian physics, a void contains nothing; the void of the international system as it truly exists looks more like that of quantum theory: emptiness that contains forces and probabilities.[8]

The place of legalism within the presumed emptiness between states becomes more visible against the background of alternatives not chosen; it is easy to appreciate the importance of legalism as a normative and political structure when compared to those that don't obtain in the world as it is. Rather than legalism, humanitarianism, for instance, might govern the international system. In that case, the "international or global community may place constraints on sovereignty in the interest of protection of vulnerable entities."[9] In this condition, states might hew to the principle of responsibility to protect. Instead of following rules, fulfilling "the duty to protect communities from mass killing, women from systematic rape, and children from starvation" would be the imperative behind policy making.[10] Policies would be contested and justified on the basis of whether they promote fulfillment of this duty. Or states might try paternalism, the "mixture of care and control" by which outsiders decide what people need or deserve and then undertake to provide it.[11] Colonialism is yet another alternative. To replace legalism, any of these or other ideas would have to occupy a place in international politics such that appeal to them was decisive in distinguishing between politically acceptable and unacceptable forms of behavior.

We do not live in any of these worlds. In fact, these concepts have been subsumed under the global legalist imperium in the sense that they have been turned into legal categories. Colonialism is understood today as inherently illegal, although the nineteenth- and twentieth-century European pioneers of international law viewed it as legally unproblematic.[12] And in the hands of the Security Council, the responsibility to protect has been subordinated to international legalism. Rather than provide an extralegal justification for war, the responsibility to protect has become one of several legal rationales for intervention under Chapter VII of the UN Charter.[13] Paternalism too has been legalized, as Stephen Hopgood shows in his study of the campaign against genital cutting.[14]

To say that interstate politics is legalistic is not to affirm that states always follow international law or that violations of law are always punished. Neither is the case. But the hegemony of the international rule of law is not manifest in compliance. It is manifest in the universality of law as a source of justification and contestation. States cannot opt out in favor of some other logic of justification. There is simply no alternative to legalism.

In this sense, law is sovereign, which means, according to Robert Paul Wolff, that it is the "supreme authority" centralized in a legal-political institution.[15] In the case of the international system, the relevant legal-political institution is a network of global-governance instruments that form what Chimni calls a kind of "global state."[16] Wendt imagines something similar as "the world state"—a "universal supranational authority" based on "a procedure for making binding and legitimate decisions about the exercise of common power."[17] All these images conjure the same idea: an international political environment structured according to overarching principles that create the possibilities for action within it.

Law is an empire not only because it governs all states' choices but also in the sense that Ikenberry has in mind: "a hierarchical order in which a powerful state engages in organized rule over several dispersed weaker and secondary polities."[18] Law facilitates empire in this traditional sense because strong states, in particular, shape the meaning of international rules and obligations through interpretation and practice.[19] Their prerogative is sometimes ratified by a type of informal consensus—as with the law on self-defense—and sometimes rejected, as with the Bush administration's definition of torture. The will of the powerful may enjoy only ambiguous legal standing, as with the practice of humanitarian intervention lacking Security Council approval.[20] But in all these situations, law is malleable in the hands of powerful states.[21] The Great Powers enjoy veto power at the Council. Big states set the agendas of multilateral conferences. The choices of "important" governments have stronger impact on interpretation of customary law. Through these and other means, the legal system tends to evolve along with the changing desires of strong governments, effectively instituting their rule over other nominally sovereign states.

So Ikenberry is right to argue that in contemporary international legal politics, the strongest states are expected to operate within as opposed to above the rules.[22] But this doesn't set law apart from the political power of empire. The strong can accomplish their goals *by use of* the rules.[23] It is hardly controversial to claim that law is a political structure through which powerful states govern with an eye toward their own interests. Throughout the rule-of-law era in world politics, the special influence of Great Powers in institutional design and legal interpretation has been readily accepted.[24]

If law is constitutive, constraining, and permissive then it certainly should not be seen through enchanted lenses. As we saw earlier, international law is often seen as being naturally associated with international order and stability, and perhaps the possibility of global human society itself.[25] Law is supposed to benefit everyone; in a happy coincidence of interests, it apparently produces no losers, only winners.[26] But this is not what legalism actually achieves. The rule of law prioritizes faithfulness to the rules as they exist over other forms of reasoning or judgment, biasing outcomes toward the accrued preferences of strong states as expressed in legal forms.

What is more, legalism tends to displace questions of politics and morality, forcing us to further question the enchanted liberal view. Where law reigns, the language, institutions, and resources of contestation are not moral and political but legal. As Shklar puts it, "Law is endowed with its own discrete, integral history, its own 'science' and its own values, which are treated as . . . sealed off from general social history, from general social theory, from politics, from morality."[27] Honig points out that, under these conditions, disagreements about what to do are turned into "juridical, administrative, or regulative tasks"—the warrant of courts and bureaucrats rather than democratic politics.[28] Hannah Arendt explored the moral implications that follow from a political system built on legal reasoning to the exclusion of political and moral thinking.[29] What all these authors urge, in their own way, is that rule following doesn't assure any particular substantive outcome. It doesn't make the world better on its own and may in fact provide a means by which to ignore the world in favor of legal words, leading to coercion, inequality, and destruction.

The "vocabulary of virtue," as Venzke calls it, around international law is hard to sustain given international legalism's bias toward strong states.[30] The procedural commitment to pacta sunt servanda reinforces and obscures a political hierarchy by ensuring that differences of power and interest are domesticated by legalization. Oona Hathaway implicitly recognizes as much when she says that "by working to . . . expand international law, the United States can also project its interests and values abroad without the use of force."[31] Thomas Friedman talks of "the hidden fist that keeps the world safe," and Stephen Brooks and William Wohlforth note that "where there are a multitude of potential cooperative scenarios," US military threats "not mentioned openly but present in the back of statemen's minds" are useful to US diplomats and negotiators. They say this "promote[s] cooperation."[32] Legalism and violence begin to look like substitutable means to accomplish the goals of US foreign policy.

Friedrich List, the nineteenth-century political economist, made an analogous observation about the politics and ideology of free trade in his time. Britain, he noted, built its industrial capacity through subsidies and protected markets, and then used the level-playing-field rhetoric of free trade to deny Germany and other rising powers the same opportunities. The apparently neutral call to follow the rules of free trade was British political exigency in disguise.[33] Today, the universal call for rule following can mask an endorsement of the rule makers' prerogative.

We should not therefore conclude that international law is inherently bad or good. We should side with neither the Trump administration, which presents global institutions as enemies, nor the editorial page of the *New York Times*, which asserts that Great Powers have a "special responsibility to uphold international law" against the will of an "outlaw state."[34] International legalism is not that simple. It does not merely constrain great powers such as the United States; it also lubricates their policy engines and tends to legitimize their interests. And it doesn't delineate moral right from wrong or make the world a safer place. Law, like other technologies, just provides tools that states and activists use to pursue their goals.

Wrap-up

The international rule of law has many faces. It sometimes appears as a formal obligation to comply. It can also take the form of guidance for the resolution of interstate disputes. And it appears as a normative aspiration—the foundation for a consensual world order in which orderly procedures replace coercion and domination. International law can be all these things because, at base, it is a system of governance. Once politically subordinated to law, governments are constrained and enabled; their options are shaped by the commitment to pacta sunt servanda. In theory, when law and state policy conflict, law wins.

But even this seeming limitation can in fact be liberating, as states use their understanding of law to work around its prohibitions and thereby affirm the legitimacy of their choices. The rule of law *governs* international politics, with contents that usually reflect the priorities of strong states. It is in this sense that international legalism is an empire—an inescapable, hierarchical, global political arrangement of authority that shapes the possibilities of action for its subjects.[35] It provides what Carl Schmitt called nomos: "a spatially concrete, constitutive act of order and orientation."[36]

This empire does not have founding documents or territorial boundaries, but it is visible in this book's case studies. Preceding chapters trace instances in which states have used the tools and resources constituted by international law. We can see in recent history how those resources shape and are shaped by state practice. These empirical findings counsel conceptual change. We cannot reasonably join liberals in contending that law is a naturally progressive force in world politics. Nor can we accept the realist claim that state power overwhelms international law. Law itself produces resources that states find useful; it is a source of power in which states invest.

Under the empire of international legalism, policy must be made consistent with legal obligations. But this just means that

foreign policy decisions have to come with legal reasons, and political disputes turn into arguments over what the law permits or
forbids. In theory, one cannot say what the results will be.

The real political consequences, however, are likely to favor
the powerful. Legalism diffuses the interests of the strong through
a system of apparently dispassionate rules. Leading powers, which
may be states, legal professionals, authoritative courts, or activists,
thereby determine the terms of possibility for everyone else. Governance by law in the international realm thus enforces a political
hierarchy backed by legalized coercion. One would not know it
from the logic and rhetoric of either liberal or realist international
relations theory. But the facts speak louder. Close attention to the
use of international law reveals the vastness of its empire, who
benefits, and who doesn't.

NOTES

Chapter 1: Introduction

1. On human rights abuses, see Randall Peerenboom, "Human Rights and the Rule of Law: What's the Relationship?" *Georgetown Journal of International Law* 36 (2005). On domestic dictatorship, the key resolutions authorizing military intervention in Libya emphasized Muammar Gaddafi's failures to comply with his international legal obligations as evidence of his government constituting a "threat to international peace and security" under chapter 7 of the charter. See S/RES/1970, S/RES/1973. For a classic, perhaps even a caricature, in the literature on international war, although the spirit exists widely in works from the UN Charter to contemporary US liberal internationalism and beyond, see Grenville Clark and Louis B. Sohn, *World Peace through World Law* (Piscataway, NJ: Transaction, 1960). In terms of other problems, see, for instance, the Rule of Law in Armed Conflict project of the Geneva Academy of International Humanitarian Law and Human Rights, http://www.adh-geneva.ch/RULAC/. Samuel Moyn notes the utopian vision of "an international law of human rights as the steward of utopian norms." Samuel Moyn, *The Last Utopia: Human Rights in History* (Cambridge, MA: Belknap Press, 2010), 4.

2. Anne-Marie Slaughter, "International Law and International Relations Theory," in *Interdisciplinary Perspectives on International Law and International Relations: The State of the Art*, ed. Jeffrey L. Dunoff and Mark A. Pollack (New York: Cambridge University Press, 2013), 616. Karen Alter suggests that "the deterioration of the rule of law [is] a path that only leads to chaos and predation." Karen J. Alter, "The Only Way to Counter Russia," usnews.com, March 12, 2014. Vladimir Putin also asserts, "[We] believe that preserving law and order in today's complex and turbulent world is one of the few ways to keep international relations from sliding into chaos. The law is still the law, and we must follow it whether we like it or not." Quoted in "A Plea for Caution from Russia," *New York Times*, September 11, 2013. For a useful summary of the growing literature on "legalization" in world politics, see Jeffrey L. Dunoff and Mark A. Pollack, eds., *Interdisciplinary Perspectives on International Law and International Relations: The State of the Art* (New York: Cambridge University Press, 2013). See also Judith L. Goldstein, Miles Kahler, Robert O. Keohane, and Anne-Marie Slaughter, eds., *Legalization and World Politics* (Cambridge, MA: MIT Press, 2001).

3. See www.unrol.org; UN Secretary-General, "Strengthening and Coordinating United Nations Rule of Law Activities," A/63/226, August 6, 2008. On the UN activi-

ties, see Alberto Cutillo, "Advancing the Rule of Law Agenda in the 67th General Assembly," International Peace Institute Policy Paper, September 17, 2012, accessed September 20, 2012, http://bit.ly/UkW36a.

4. Keally McBride, *Mr. Mothercountry: The Man Who Made the Rule of Law* (Oxford: Oxford University Press, 2016), 161.

5. See also Shirley V. Scott, "International Law as Ideology: Theorizing the Relationship between International Law and International Politics," *European Journal of International Law* 5, no. 3 (1994): 313–25; Jeremy Waldron, "The Rule of International Law," *Harvard Journal of Law and Public Policy* 30, no. 1 (2006): 15–30; Simon Chesterman, "An International Rule of Law?" *American Journal of Comparative Law* 56, no. 2 (2008): 331–61; Ingo Venzke, *How Interpretation Makes International Law* (Oxford: Oxford University Press, 2012); Friedrich V. Kratochwil, *The Status of Law in World Society: Meditations on the Role and Rule of Law* (Cambridge: Cambridge University Press, 2014). See also Keally McBride, *Mr. Mothercountry: The Man Who Made the Rule of Law* (Oxford: Oxford University Press, 2016), 161.

6. By international law, I mean the formal obligations of classical interstate public international law. These commitments are legally binding on governments in their relations with other governments and therefore contain the possibility of violation in a formal sense. This body of commitments is different from other kinds of commitments, such as soft law, voluntary standards, norms, and shared expectations, that states may take on but that do not include formal legal obligations. Soft law and norms may well be influential in world politics, but my interest is in the distinctive politics around formal legal obligations along with their politics of compliance and violation. This requires narrowing my focus to formal legal commitments, and setting aside norms and soft law.

7. Beth A. Simmons, *Mobilizing for Human Rights: International Law in Domestic Politics* (Cambridge: Cambridge University Press, 2009), 5.

8. See, for instance, W. Michael Reisman, "Self-Defense in an Age of Terrorism," Faculty Scholarship Series, Yale Law School, no. 105, 2003, accessed September 13, 2016, http://digitalcommons.law.yale.edu/cgi/viewcontent.cgi?article=2040 &context=fss_papers.

9. Lassa Oppenheim, "The Science of International Law: Its Task and Method," *American Journal of International Law* 2 (1908): 313, cited in Matt Craven, "Introduction: International Law and Its Histories," in *Time, History, and International Law*, ed. Matthew Craven, Malgosia Fitzmaurice, and Maria Vogiatzi (Leiden: Brill 2007), 1. The Vienna Convention on the Law of Treaties (1969) notes "the ever-increasing importance of treaties as a source of international law and as a means of developing peaceful cooperation among nations."

10. G. John Ikenberry, *Liberal Leviathan: The Origins, Crisis, and Transformation of the American World Order* (Princeton, NJ: Princeton University Press, 2011). For an excellent account of international legal debates and justifications around World War I, see Isabell Hull, *A Scrap of Paper: Breaking and Making International Law during the Great War* (Ithaca, NY: Cornell University Press, 2014). In policy debates on Syria's

chemical weapons in 2013 and Russia's takeover of Crimea in 2014, see Ian Hurd, "On Law, Policy, and (Not) Bombing Syria," accessed April 1, 2014, http://bit.ly/1gltm0r; Chris Borgen, "From Intervention to Recognition: Russia, Crimea, and Arguments over Recognizing Secessionist Entities," accessed April 1, 2014, http://bit.ly/1pI0aGk; Alter, "The Only Way to Counter Russia."

11. John H. Jackson, *The World Trading System: Law and Policy of International Economic Relations*, 2nd ed. (Cambridge, MA: MIT Press, 1997), 110.

12. Statement of April 30, 1959, cited in William W. Bishop, "The International Rule of Law," *Michigan Law Review* 59 (1961): 555.

13. On the Lockean analogy, see John Gerard Ruggie, "Continuity and Transformation in the World Polity," *World Politics* 35, no. 2 (1983): 261–85.

14. It is common but facile to conclude therefore that international law is insignificant; see, for instance, Jack L. Goldsmith and Eric A. Posner, *The Limits of International Law* (Oxford: Oxford University Press, 2005); John Mearsheimer, "The False Promise of International Institutions," *International Security* 19, no. 3 (1994–95): 5–49. More interesting are scholars who recognize this "weakness" but then go on to figure out how it fits with the significant role of international law in public diplomacy and the internal deliberations of states. Among these, see Andrew Guzman, *How International Law Works: A Rational Choice Theory* (Oxford: Oxford University Press, 2010); Jutta Brunnée and Stephen J. Toope, *Legitimacy and Legality in International Law: An Interactional Account* (Cambridge: Cambridge University Press, 2010); Kratochwil, *The Status of Law in World Society*.

15. See, for instance, Guzman, *How International Law Works*.

16. See, for instance, Jothie Rajah, " 'Rule of Law' as a Transnational Legal Order," in *Transnational Legal Orders*, ed. Terence C. Halliday and Gregory Shaffer (New York: Cambridge University Press, 2015); Charlotte Peevers, *The Politics of Justifying Force: The Suez Crisis, the Iraq War, and International Law* (Oxford: Oxford University Press, 2013).

17. See, though, Nathaniel Berman, "Privileging Combat? Contemporary Conflict and the Legal Construction of War," *Columbia Journal of Transnational Law* 43 (2004–5): 1–71.

18. This point is implicit in Peevers, *The Politics of Justifying Force*; Jens David Ohlin, *The Assault on International Law* (Oxford: Oxford University Press, 2015).

19. See http://bit.ly/1kpdaz3 (accessed April 1, 2014).

20. See Mara Pillinger, Ian Hurd, and Michael N. Barnett, "How to Get Away with Cholera: The UN, Haiti, and International Law," *Perspectives on Politics* 14, no. 1 (March 2016): 70–86.

21. Scott, "International Law as Ideology."

22. A survey of this approach might begin with the International Law Commission's mandate for codification and the "progressive development" of international law, and continue through to the "rational design" movement in IR scholarship in the 2000s.

23. For a fine example, see Guzman, *How International Law Works*.

24. See also Venzke, *How Interpretation Makes International Law*.

25. Stephen D. Krasner, *Sovereignty: Organized Hypocrisy* (Princeton, NJ: Princeton University Press, 1999).

26. In *The Limits of International Law*, Jack Goldsmith and Eric Posner exemplify the split between nonlaw "interests" and postlaw "cooperation." They begin by assuming that states follow only their interests (and do not have an inherent preference for compliance over noncompliance with law). This requires the ability to see interests as distinct from and prior to international law. See also Guzman *How International Law Works*.

27. Compare, for instance, H. J. Morgenthau ("When there is neither community interest nor balance of power, there is no international law") with G. John Ikenberry. H. J. Morgenthau, "Positivism, Functionalism, and International Law," *American Journal of International Law* 34 (1940): 274; Ikenberry, *Liberal Leviathan*.

28. See, for example, Ruti G. Teitel, *Humanity's Law* (Oxford: Oxford University Press, 2011), 3.

29. Nico Krisch, "International Law in Times of Hegemony," *European Journal of International Law* 16, no. 2 (2005): 369–408.

30. See, for instance, Henry R. Nau, *Conservative Internationalism: Armed Diplomacy under Jefferson, Polk, Truman, and Reagan* (Princeton, NJ: Princeton University Press, 2013); Yan Xuetong, *Ancient Chinese Thought, Modern Chinese Power* (Princeton, NJ: Princeton University Press, 2011); Stephen G. Brooks and William C. Wohlforth, *World Out of Balance: International Relations and the Challenge of American Primacy* (Princeton, NJ: Princeton University Press, 2008).

31. Stephen G. Brooks and William C. Wohlforth, *America Abroad: The United States' Global Role in the 21st Century* (Oxford: Oxford University Press, 2016).

32. Benno Teschke, *The Myth of 1648: Class, Geopolitics, and the Making of Modern International Relations* (London: Verso, 2003).

33. Charlotte Epstein, *The Power of Words in International Relations: Birth of an Anti-Whaling Discourse* (Cambridge, MA: MIT Press, 2008); Ian Hurd, "Almost Saving Whales: The Ambiguity of Success at the International Whaling Commission," *Ethics and International Affairs* 26, no. 1 (2012): 103–12.

34. Guzman, *How International Law Works*. See also Ohlin, *The Assault on International Law*.

35. Benedict Kinsgbury, "The International Legal Order," Public Law Research Paper, New York University School of Law, 01–04, 2003, 17.

36. Charles J. Dunlap Jr., "Law and Military Interventions: Preserving Humanitarian Values in 21st Century Conflicts," Kennedy School of Government Working Papers, 2001.

37. See, for instance, thelawfareproject.org (accessed May 11, 2012). This is similar to Brian Tamanaha's complaint about the "political" uses of domestic law "as a means to an end" as opposed to other, more legitimate uses of law. Brian Z. Tamanaha, *Law as a Means to an End: Threat to the Rule of Law* (Cambridge: Cambridge University Press, 2006). Hauke Brunkhorst notes this effect but sees the opposite political out-

come, celebrating the emancipatory power of international law for weak states. Hauke Brunkhorst, *Critical Theory of Legal Revolutions: Evolutionary Perspectives* (London: Bloomsbury, 2014). He does not provide any empirical evidence that this emancipatory potential is realized with much frequency in the world as it is.

38. On international rules and Chinese foreign policy, see Ikenberry, *Liberal Leviathan*.

39. Ian Shapiro, *The Evolution of Rights in Liberal Theory* (Cambridge: Cambridge University Press, 1986), 100.

40. Rosa Brooks, "All the Pentagon's Lawyers," *Foreign Policy*, August 29, 2012, accessed September 20, 2012, http://bit.ly/PRfdga.

41. On the "political productivity of law's ambiguity," see Iza Hussin, "Circulations of Law: Cosmopolitan Elites, Global Repertoires, Local Vernaculars," *Law and History Review* 32, no. 4 (2014): 773–95.

42. Bernard Harcourt, *The Illusion of Free Markets: Punishment and the Myth of Natural Order* (Cambridge, MA: Harvard University Press, 2012).

43. Helen Kinsella, *The Image before the Weapon: A Critical History of the Distinction between Combatant and Civilian* (Ithaca, NY: Cornell University Press, 2011).

44. Ibid., 7.

45. For an example of this exercise, see Harold Koh, "The Obama Administration and International Law" (address to the annual meeting of the American Society of International Law, Washington, DC, 2010).

46. See, among others, Rosa Brooks, "Duck-Rabbits and Drones: Legal Indeterminacy in the War on Terror," *Stanford Law and Policy Review* 25 (2013): 301–16; Ohlin, *The Assault on International Law*.

47. In international law and politics, see Janina Dill, *Legitimate Targets? Social Construction, International Law, and US Bombing* (Cambridge: Cambridge University Press, 2015); Peevers, *The Politics of Justifying Force*. In other settings, see Iza Hussin, "Circulations of Law"; Benjamin Schonthal, *Buddhism, Politics, and the Limits of Law* (New York: Cambridge University Press, 2016).

48. See, for instance, Mary Ellen O'Connell, "War and Peace," in *The Oxford Handbook of the History of International Law*, ed. Bardo Fassbender and Anne Peters (Oxford: Oxford University Press, 2012), 272–93.

49. See the Prosecutor v. Anto Furundzija decision of the International Criminal Tribunal for the Former Yugoslavia. See also the discussion in Erika de Wet, "The Prohibition of Torture as an International Norm of *jus cogens* and Its Implications for National and Customary Law," *European Journal of International Law* 15, no. 1 (2004): 97–121.

50. Harold Hongju Koh made an excellent critique in his testimony to the US Senate confirmation hearings for Alberto Gonzales as US attorney general in 2005. See https://www.judiciary.senate.gov/imo/media/doc/koh_testimony_01_06_05.pdf (accessed September 15, 2016).

51. Scott Veitch, *Law and Irresponsibility: On the Legitimation of Human Suffering* (Abingdon, UK: Routledge-Cavendish, 2007).

Chapter 2: The Rule of Law, Domestic and International

1. I am interested here in hard versus soft law. My focus on the politics of compliance and noncompliance requires that we look at rules for which it is conceptually possible to violate, and this requires exploring the binding legal obligations of states. For excellent resources on the distinction between these two kinds of rules, see Kenneth W. Abbott and Duncan Snidal, "Hard and Soft Law in International Governance," *International Organization* 54, no. 3 (2000): 421–55; Emilie Hafner-Burton, David G. Victor, and Yonatan Lupu, "Political Science Research on International Law: The State of the Field," *American Journal of International Law* 106, no. 1 (2012): 47–97; Alain Pellet, "The Normative Dilemma: Will and Consent in International Law-Making," *Australian Yearbook of International Law* (1988): 22–53. Pellet argues that it is insufficient to see international law as primarily a body of hard laws underpinned by state consent.

2. Jeremy Matam Farrall, *United Nations Sanctions and the Rule of Law* (Cambridge: Cambridge University Press, 2007), 39. See also Rosa Brooks, "All the Pentagon's Lawyers," *Foreign Policy*, August 29, 2012, accessed March 4, 2017, http://foreignpolicy.com/2012/08/29/all-the-pentagons-lawyers/.

3. In this large literature, see, for instance, Brian Z. Tamanaha, *On the Rule of Law: History, Politics, Theory* (Cambridge: Cambridge University Press, 2004); Joseph Raz, "The Rule of Law and Its Virtue," *Law Quarterly Review* 93 (1977): 198; Tom Bingham, *The Rule of Law* (London: Penguin, 2001); Tom Ginsburg and Tamir Moustafa, eds., *Rule by Law: The Politics of Courts in Authoritarian Regimes* (Cambridge: Cambridge University Press, 2008).

4. Tamanaha, *On the Rule of Law*, chap. 9.

5. Simon Chesterman, "An International Rule of Law?" *American Journal of Comparative Law* 56, no. 2 (Spring 2008): 337. Friedrich Hayek provides a similar list, with the important addition of a substantive list of rights without which he believes the rule of law cannot exist. Friedrich Hayek, *The Constitution of Liberty* (Abingdon, UK: Routledge, 1960).

6. Lon Fuller, *Morality of Law* (New Haven, CT: Yale University Press, 1969). See also Colleen Murphy, "Lon Fuller and the Moral Value of the Rule of Law," *Law and Philosophy* 24, no. 3 (May 2005): 239–62; Jutta Brunnée and Stephen J. Toope, *Legitimacy and Legality in International Law: An Interactional Account* (Cambridge: Cambridge University Press, 2010).

7. *World Justice Project Rule of Law Index*, accessed July 12, 2012, http://www.worldjusticeproject.org/rule-of-law-index/.

8. Raz, "The Rule of Law and its Virtue," 198.

9. Friedrich Hayek, *The Political Ideal of the Rule of Law* (1955), cited in Laura Greenfell, *Promoting the Rule of Law in Post-Conflict Societies* (Cambridge: Cambridge University Press, Cambridge, 2013), 69.

10. Raz, "The Rule of Law and Its Virtue," 214 (emphasis added).

11. Tamanaha, *On the Rule of Law*, 114.

12. A. V. Dicey, *An Introduction to the Study of the Law (1885/1945)*, cited in Bingham, *The Rule of Law*, 4.

13. Karen J. Alter, *The New Terrain of International Law: Court, Politics, Rights* (Princeton, NJ: Princeton University Press, 2013), 340.

14. Tamir Moustafa and Tom Ginsburg, "Introduction: The Function of Courts in Authoritarian Politics," in *Rule by Law: The Politics of Courts in Authoritarian Regimes*, ed. Tom Ginsburg and Tamir Moustafa (Cambridge: Cambridge University Press, 2008), 1–22.

15. Tamanaha, *On the Rule of Law*, 126.

16. Raz, "The Rule of Law and Its Virtue," 200.

17. See, for instance, Scott Veitch, *Law and Irresponsibility: On the Legitimation of Human Suffering* (Abingdon, UK: Routledge-Cavendish, 2007). In international settings, see Gerry Simpson, *Great Power and Outlaw States: Unequal Sovereigns in the International Legal Order* (Cambridge: Cambridge University Press, 2004).

18. Raz, "The Rule of Law and Its Virtue," 201.

19. John P. McCormick, "Identifying or Exploiting the Paradoxes of Constitutional Democracy: An Introduction to Carl Schmitt's Legality and Legitimacy," in *Legality and Legitimacy*, by Carl Schmitt, trans. Jeffrey Seitzer (Durham, NC: Duke University Press, 2004), xiii–xliii.

20. See, among others, the historical narrative in Bingham, *The Rule of Law*.

21. Paul Johnson, "Laying Down the Law, " *Wall Street Journal*, March 10, 1999. In contrast, for a useful distinction between the rule of law and a democratic political order, and an assertion that the requirements of the rule of law and democracy can conflict, see Michel Rosenfeld, "The Rule of Law and the Legitimacy of Constitutional Democracy," *Southern California Law Review* 74 (2001): 1307–52. See also the UN Rule of Law project, https://www.un.org/ruleoflaw/ (accessed March 4, 2017); Thomas Carothers, ed., *Promoting the Rule of Law Abroad: In Search of Knowledge* (Washington, DC: Carnegie Endowment for International Peace, 2006); Farrall, *United Nations Sanctions and the Rule of Law*; Brian Z. Tamanaha, *Law as a Means to an End: The Threat to the Rule of Law* (Cambridge: Cambridge University Press, 2006), 2, chap. 12.

22. See, for instance, Allen Buchanan, *Justice, Legitimacy, and Self-Determination: Moral Foundations for International Law* (Oxford: Oxford University Press, 2007). For empirical connections between legitimacy and law, see Tom R. Tyler, *Why People Obey the Law* (Princeton, NJ: Princeton University Press, 2006). See also Ronald Dworkin, *Law's Empire* (Cambridge, MA: Belknap Press, 1986).

23. Raz, "The Rule of Law and Its Virtue," 196.

24. Lon Fuller, 1975, cited in Tamanaha, *On the Rule of Law*, 95.

25. Compare Tamanaha, *On the Rule of Law*; introduction to Ginsburg and Moustafa, *Rule by Law*.

26. These themes are raised in Antje Wiener, Anthony F. Lang Jr., James Tully, Miguel Poiares Maduro, and Mattias Kumm, "Global Constitutionalism: Human Rights, Democracy, and the Rule of Law," *Global Constitutionalism* 1 (2012): 1–15.

27. On the first, see, for instance, Thomas M. Franck, "What, Eat the Cabin Boy? Uses of Force That Are Illegal but Justifiable,' in *Recourse to Force: State Action against Threats and Armed Attacks* (Cambridge: Cambridge University Press, 2002); Bruno Simma, "NATO, the UN, and the Use of Force: Legal Aspects," *European Journal of International Law* 10 (1999): 1–22. On the second, see the literature on *jus cogens*, including Erika de Wet, "The Prohibition on Torture as an International Norm of *Jus Cogens* and Its Implications for National and Customary Law," *European Journal of International Law* 15, no. 1 (2004): 97–121. On Schmitt's "community will," see Carl Schmitt, *Legality and Legitimacy*, trans. Jeffrey Seitzer (Durham, NC: Duke University Press, 2004).

28. Raz, "The Rule of Law and Its Virtue," 209 (emphasis added).

29. "The Rule of Law and Transitional Justice in Conflict and Post-Conflict Societies," UN secretary-general report, S/2004/616, para. 6.

30. Bingham, *The Rule of Law*, 9.

31. As George Downs, David Rocke, and Peter Barsoom say, "Instances of apparent noncompliance are problems to be solved, rather than violations that have to be punished." George W. Downs, David M. Rocke, and Peter N. Barsoom, "Is the Good News about Compliance Goods News about Cooperation?" *International Organization* 50, no. 3 (July 1996): 381.

32. Judith Goldstein, Miles Kahler, Robert O. Keohane, and Anne-Marie Slaughter, "Introduction: Legalization and World Politics," *International Organization* 54, no. 3 (2000): 386.

33. Martti Koskenniemi, *The Gentle Civilizer of Nations: The Rise and Fall of International Law, 1870–1960* (Cambridge: Cambridge University Press, 2001); Martti Koskenniemi, "The Advantage of Treaties: International Law in the Enlightenment," *Edinburgh Law Review* 13 (2009): 27–67.

34. Case of the SS *Lotus* (France v. Turkey), judgment of September 7, 1927, PCIJ Series A, No. 10, 18.

35. Theresa Reinold and Michael Zürn, "'Rules about Rules' and the Endogenous Dynamics of International Law: Dissonance Reduction as a Mechanism of Secondary Rule-Making," *Global Constitutionalism* 3, no. 2 (2014): 236.

36. See, for instance, the UN Charter; "The Role of the United Nations in International Law," UN Fact Sheet no. 2, 2012, accessed December 19, 2012, http://treaties.un.org/doc/source/events/2012/Press_kit/fact_sheet_2_english.pdf.

37. UN General Assembly Resolution 174, 1947, A/RES/174(II).

38. Secretary-general's letter to heads of state and government, May 9, 2012, accessed September 20, 2012, http://bit.ly/QFvrcF.

39. Goldstein et al., "Introduction: Legalization and World Politics," 387.

40. Thomas M. Franck, *The Power of Legitimacy among Nations* (Oxford: Oxford University Press, 1990), 52, 53.

41. Ibid. See also Reinold and Zürn, "Rules about Rules."

42. Franck, 54. On the "managerial school" in international law, see Abram Chayes and Antonia Handler Chayes, *The New Sovereignty: Compliance with International Regulatory Agreements* (Cambridge, MA: Harvard University Press, 1998).

43. Although several states have challenged the legality of Iceland's position, and thus the legal issue at the heart of this example is contested.

44. This is true with respect to the International Whaling Convention. There can be other limits in other treaties to which Turkey is a party, including the Convention on International Trade in Endangered Species of Wild Fauna and Flora, which regulates the international trade in many whale parts.

45. Frederic L. Kirgis, "North Korea's Withdrawal from the Nuclear Nonproliferation Treaty," *insights*, January 24, 2003, accessed March 5, 2017, https://www.asil.org/insights/volume/8/issue/2/north-koreas-withdrawal-nuclear-nonproliferation-treaty.

46. See https://treaties.un.org/doc/publication/unts/volume%201155/volume-1155-i-18232-english.pdf (accessed April 14, 2017).

47. Laurence R. Helfer, "Exiting Treaties," *Virginia Law Review* 91, no. 7 (2005): 1579–648.

48. See David A. Coulson, "How Persistent Must the Persistent Objector Be?" *Washington Law Review* 61 (1986): 958–59. For a critique of the concept of the persistent objector, see Patrick Dumberry, "Incoherent and Ineffective: The Concept of the Persistent Objector Revisited," *International and Comparative Law Quarterly* 59 (2010): 779–802.

49. More recent claims have been made for the norm against torture (such as Prosecutor v. Anto Furundzija in the International Criminal Tribunal for the Former Yugoslavia case).

50. On the Democratic Republic of Congo v. Rwanda case, see para. 64, accessed March 5, 2017, http://humanrightsdoctorate.blogspot.nl/2012/07/antigone-jus-cogens-and-international.html. Case concerning East Timor (Portugal v. Australia), ICJ Reports 1995. See the discussion in Matthew Saul, "The Normative Status of Self-Determination in International Law: A Formula for Uncertainty in the Scope and Content of the Right?" *Human Rights Law Review* 11, no. 4 (2011): 609–44.

51. Judge Antônio Augusto Cançado Trindade's strong statement that the ban on torture is a peremptory norm of international law is offset by Judge Ronny Abraham's, among others, less conclusive statements. See http://humanrightsdoctorate.blogspot.nl/2012/07/antigone-jus-cogens-and-international.html (accessed March 5, 2017). At the International Criminal Tribunal for the Former Yugoslavia, see Prosecutor v. Anto Furundzija (1998).

52. On the autonomy of the legal sphere, see, for instance, Reinold and Zürn, "Rules about Rules." On law as superordinate, see Bingham, *The Rule of Law*. On individual liberty, see F. A. Hayek, *The Constitution of Liberty: The Definitive Edition* (Chicago: University of Chicago Press, 2011).

53. Jeremy Waldron, "Are Sovereigns Entitled to the Benefit of the Rule of Law?" *European Journal of International Law* 22, no. 2 (2011): 315–43.

54. Kenneth N. Waltz, *Theory of International Politics* (Hoboken, NJ: Wiley, 1979); Hedley Bull, *The Anarchical Society: A Study in World Order*, 3rd ed. (New York: Columbia University Press, 2002); Alexander E. Wendt, *Social Theory of International Politics* (Cambridge: Cambridge University Press, 1999); Richard K. Ashley, "Untying

the Sovereign State: A Double Reading of the Anarchy Problematique," *Millennium* 17 (1988): 227–62.

55. For the classic framing, see Robert O. Keohane, *After Hegemony: Cooperation and Discord in the World Political Economy* (Princeton, NJ: Princeton University Press, 1984).

56. Immanuel Kant, "To Perpetual Peace: A Philosophic Sketch, 1795," trans. Ted Humphrey, in *Perpetual Peace and Other Essays* (Indianapolis: Hackett, 1983), sec. 354.

57. Tim Büthe and Walter Mattli, *The New Global Rulers: The Privatization of Regulation in the World Economy* (Princeton, NJ: Princeton University Press, 2013); David A. Lake, *Hierarchy in International Relations* (Ithaca, NY: Cornell University Press, 2009); Simpson, *Great Powers and Outlaw States*; Louis W. Pauly and Edgar Grande, "Reconstituting Political Authority: Sovereignty, Effectiveness, and Legitimacy in a Transnational Legal Order," in *Complex Sovereignty: Reconstituting Political Authority in the Twenty-First Century*, ed. Edgar Grande and Louis W. Pauly (Toronto: University of Toronto Press, 2005); B. S. Chimni, "International Institutions Today: An Imperial Global State in the Making," *European Journal of International Law* 15, no. 1 (2004): 1–37. On other legitimated international institutions, see, for instance, the UN Security Council; Ian Hurd, *After Anarchy: Legitimacy and Power in the UN Security Council* (Princeton, NJ: Princeton University Press, 2007).

58. Harold Hongju Koh, "Transnational Public Law Litigation," *Yale Law Journal* 100 (1991): 2372–402.

59. Helen Milner, "The Assumption of Anarchy in International Politics: A Critique," *Review of International Studies* 17, no. 1 (1991): 67–85; Hurd, *After Anarchy*.

60. James N. Rosenau and Ernst-Otto Czempiel, *Governance without Government: Order and Change in World Politics* (Cambridge: Cambridge University Press 1992).

61. The literature on the special role of Great Powers, singly or collectively, in generating international order is large and varied. It includes classical writings on Great Power politics, such as Hans J. Morgenthau, *Politics among Nations* (New York: Alfred A. Knopf, 1973); E. H. Carr, *The Twenty-Years Crisis, 1919–1939* (London: Macmillan, 1939); Hedley Bull, *The Anarchical Society: A Study in World Order* (New York: Columbia University Press, 1977). It also encompasses significant strands of writing on the needs of US foreign policy, such as G. John Ikenberry, *After Victory: Institutions, Strategic Restraint, and the Rebuilding of Order after Major Wars* (Princeton, NJ: Princeton University Press, 2001); Bruce Jones, Carlos Pascual, and Stephen John Stedman, *Power and Responsibility: Building International Order in an Era of Transnational Threats* (Washington, DC: Brookings Institution Press, 2009). A more critical variant sees it as an aspect of hegemony or empire: Simpson, *Great Powers and Outlaw States*; Rosemary Foot, S. Neil MacFarlane, and Michael Mastanduno, *US Hegemony and International Organizations* (Oxford: Oxford University Press, 2003); Michael Byers and Georg Nolte, *United States Hegemony and the Foundations of International Law* (Cambridge: Cambridge University Press, 2003); Michael Hardt and Antonio Negri, *Empire* (Cambridge, MA: Harvard University Press, 2000).

62. Sidney D. Bailey, "New Light on Abstentions in the UN Security Council," *International Affairs* 50, no. 4 (1974): 554–73.

63. South Africa's argument does suggest that the consensus is something short of universal, or at least that there remains an opening for the strategic use of its complaint when it serves its interests. On informal Charter amendments, see Ian Hurd, "Security Council Reform: Informal Membership and Practice," in *The Once and Future Security Council*, ed. Bruce M. Russett (New York: St. Martin's Press, 1997).

64. Christine Grey, *International Law and the Use of Force* (Oxford: Oxford University Press, 2004). Compare to Thomas M. Franck, "What, Eat the Cabin Boy?"

65. Ian Hurd, "The UN Security Council and the International Rule of Law," *Chinese Journal of International Politics* 7, no. 3 (2014): 361–79.

66. On the constitutional status of the Charter, see Michael W. Doyle, "The UN Charter—A Global Constitution?" in *Ruling the World? Constitutionalism, International Law, and Global Governance*, ed. Jeffrey L. Dunoff and Joel P. Trachtman (New York: Cambridge University Press 2009), 113–32.

67. Hurd *After Anarchy*, chap. 7.

68. The binding quality of Council decisions is established at the intersection of Articles 25 and 39 of the Charter. See also Farrall, *United Nations Sanctions and the Rule of Law*. On the Council's move into something resembling global legislation, see Ian Johnstone, "The UN Security Council as Legislature," in *The UN Security Council and the Politics of International Authority*, ed. Bruce Cronin and Ian Hurd (Abingdon, UK: Routledge, 2008), 80–104.

69. On the early days, see Ruth B. Russell, *A History of the United Nations Charter: The Role of the United States, 1940–1945* (Washington, DC: Brookings Institution Press, 1958). For later practice, see Farrall, *United Nations Sanctions and the Rule of Law*. On Kadi, see Conor Gearty, "In Praise of Awkwardness: Kadi in the CJEU," *European Constitutional Law Review* 10, no. 1 (2014): 15–27.

70. On the distinction between legal and political matters in the United Nations, see Rosalyn Higgins, *The Development of International Law through the Political Organs of the United Nations* (Oxford: Oxford University Press, 1963); Steven R. Ratner, "The Security Council and International Law," in *The UN Security Council: From the Cold War to the 21st Century*, ed. David M. Malone (Boulder, CO: Lynne Rienner, 2004), 591–605.

71. Hans Kelsen, *The Law of the United Nations* (Clark, NJ: Lawbook Exchange, 2000); Farrall, *United Nations Sanctions and the Rule of Law*, chap. 1.

72. José E. Alvarez, "Contemporary International Law: An 'Empire of Law' or the 'Law of Empire,'" *American University International Law Review* 24, no. 5 (2008): 811–42; Ian Hurd, "UN Security Council," in *The Oxford Handbook of International Security*, ed. Alexandra Gheciu and William C. Wohlforth (Oxford: Oxford University Press, 2017).

73. See, for instance, José E. Alvarez, "Judging the Security Council," *American Journal of International Law* 90, no. 1 (1996): 1–39.

74. José E. Alvarez, *International Organizations as Law-Makers* (Oxford: Oxford University Press, 2005), 71.

75. Namibia ICJ Reports (1971); Kamrul Hossain, "Legality of the Security Council Action: Does the International Court of Justice Move to Take Up the Challenge of Judicial Review?" *Uluslararasi Hukuk ve Politika* 5, 17 (2009): 133–63. One element of the Lockerbie dispute was the claim by Libya that the Council acted ultra vires in imposing economic sanctions against it even after Libya satisfied the obligation under the Montreal Convention on the Suppression of Unlawful Acts against the Safety of Civil Aviation (1971) related to air terrorism. This provided the Court the opportunity to review the legality of Council's resolutions 731 and 748.

76. "Summary of the Summary of the Judgment of 27 February 1998," accessed March 6, 2017, http://www.icj-cij.org/docket/index.php?sum=460&p1=3&p2=3&k=82&p3=5&case=88&PHPSESSID=31e7e012b66d5744748863cc574778a3.

77. See, for instance, Nico Krisch, "International Law in Times of Hegemony: Unequal Power and the Shaping of the International Legal Order," *European Journal of International Law* 16, no. 3 (2005): 369–408.

78. For customary law, state agency is preserved by the persistent objector rule. See Coulson, "How Persistent Must the Persistent Objector Be?" For a critique of the concept of the persistent objector, see Dumberry, "Incoherent and Ineffective."

79. See, for instance, Andeas L. Paulus, "The International Legal System as a Constitution," in *Ruling the World? Constitutionalism, International Law, and Global Governance*, ed. Jeffrey L. Dunoff and Joel P. Trachtman (New York: Cambridge University Press, 2009), 69–112.

80. As Koskenniemi notes, "The project of the rule of law cannot be reduced to the fidelity to the purported meaning of particular laws. . . . [W]hat laws mean and the objectives they may appear to have will depend on the judgement of the law-applier." Martti Koskenniemi, "Constitutionalism as Mindset: Reflections on Kantian Themes about International Law and Globalization," *Theoretical Inquiries in Law* 8, no. 1 (2007): 9–36.

81. See also Frédéric Mégret, discussing Koskenniemi's *From Apology to Utopia*, in "Thinking about What International Lawyers 'Do': The Laws of War as a Socio-Legal Field Structured by Apology and Utopia," in *The Law of International Lawyers: Reading Martti Koskenniemi*, ed. Wouter Werner, Marieke de Hoon, and Alexis Galán (Cambridge: Cambridge University Press, 2017), 265–96.

82. Shirley V. Scott, "International Law as Ideology: Theorizing the Relationship between International Law and International Politics," *European Journal of International Law* 5 (1994): 313–25.

83. Ian Hurd, "International Law and the Politics of Diplomacy," in *Diplomacy and the Making of World Politics*, ed. Ole Jacob Sending, Vincent Pouliot, and Iver B. Neumann (Cambridge: Cambridge University Press, 2015), 31–54.

84. "The mode of contestation, that is the way that contestation is displayed in practice, depends on the . . . environment where contestation takes place." Antje Wiener, *A Theory of Contestation* (Heidelberg: Springer, 2014), 1.

85. Mattias Kumm, Anthony F. Lang, James Tully, and Antje Wiener, "How Large Is the World of Global Constitutionalism," *Global Constitutionalism* 3, no. 1 (2014): 1.

NOTES TO CHAPTER 3 151

86. I mean instrumental here in Tamanaha's sense in *On the Rule of Law* of being implicated in the agent's interests, and not in the sense used by Koskenniemi in "Constitutionalism as Mindset." Tamanaha warns against instrumentalism, as a nefarious dangerous development, but here I suggest it is elemental to the international legal-political system.

87. This makes possible a dynamic interaction between legal resources and state interests, as outlined in Carmen Wunderlich, "Theoretical Approaches in Norm Dynamics," in *Norm Dynamics in Multilateral Arms Control: Interests, Conflicts, and Justice*, ed. Harald Müller and Carmen Wunderlich (Athens: University of Georgia Press, 2013), 20–48.

88. Charles Taylor, "To Follow a Rule . . . ," in *Bourdieu: Critical Perspectives*, ed. Craig Calhoun, Edward LiPuma, and Moishe Postone (Chicago: University of Chicago Press, 1993), 45–60.

Chapter 3: How to Do Things with International Law

1. Rosalyn Higgins, "The Identity of International Law," in *International Law: Teaching and Practice* , ed. Bin Cheng (London: Stevens and Sons, 1983), 37, cited in Shirley V. Scott, "International Law as Ideology: Theorizing the Relationship between International Law and International Politics," *European Journal of International Law* 5 (1994): 8.

2. See Heinz Klug and Sally Engle Merry, *The New Legal Realism: Studying Law Globally* (New York: Cambridge University Press, 2016). On international legal realism, see the symposium in *Leiden Journal of International Law* 28 (2015).

3. See, for instance, Louis Henkin, *How Nations Behave: Law and Foreign Policy*, 2nd ed. (New York: Columbia University Press, 1979); Abram Chayes and Antonio Handler Chayes, *The New Sovereignty: Compliance with International Regulatory Agreements* (Cambridge, MA: Harvard University Press, 1998); Thomas M. Franck, *The Power of Legitimacy among Nations* (Oxford: Oxford University Press, 1990). A wave of new scholarship has begun unpacking this idea for IR. In addition to the work cited elsewhere in this chapter, see also Anne Orford, *International Authority and the Responsibility to Protect* (Cambridge: Cambridge University Press, 2011); Friedrich V. Kratochwil, *The Status of Law in World Society: Meditations on the Role and Rule of Law* (Cambridge: Cambridge University Press, 2014); Frédéric Mégret, "What Sort of Global Justice is 'International Criminal Justice'?" *Journal of International Criminal Justice* 13 (2015): 77–96.

4. On practices, see, among others, Pierre Bourdieu, *Outline of a Theory of Practice* (Cambridge: Cambridge University Press, 1977). On IR, see Emanuel Adler and Vincent Pouliot, eds., *International Practices* (Cambridge: Cambridge University Press, 2011). On international law, see Jutta Brunnée and Stephen J. Toope, *Legitimacy and Legality in International Law: An Interactional Account* (Cambridge: Cambridge University Press, 2009); Jens Meierhenrich, "The Practice of International Law: A Theoretical Analysis," *Law and Contemporary Problems* 76, 3–4 (2013): 1–83. This is

implied also by Alexander Wendt's presentation of structurationism as a style of research. Alexander E. Wendt, "The Agent-Structure Problem in International Relations Theory," *International Organization* 41, no. 3 (1987): 335–70.

5. For instance, respectively, the Center for Justice and Accountability is among many groups gathering evidence for the International Criminal Court and others in support of prosecutions for human rights atrocities; Sea Shepherd appeals to the antiwhaling legal regime to justify its operations on the high seas; and the Coalition for the International Criminal Court encourages popular and government support for the International Criminal Court.

6. Elements of this section draw on Ian Hurd, "Law and the Practice of Diplomacy," in *Diplomacy and the Making of World Politics*, ed. Ole Jacob Sending, Vincent Pouliot, and Iver B. Neumann (Cambridge: Cambridge University Press, 2015), 31–54.

7. Marta Fernandéz Moreno, Carlos Chagas Vianna Braga, and Maíra Siman Gomes, "Trapped between Many Worlds: A Post-Colonial Perspective on the UN Mission in Haiti (MINUSTAH)," *International Peacekeeping* 19, no. 3 (2012): 377–92; "Bush: This Government Does Not Torture," CNN, October 5, 2007, accessed July 26, 2016, http://www.cnn.com/2007/POLITICS/10/05/bush.torture/index .html?iref=newssearch; Stuart Taylor Jr., "Nicaragua Takes Case against U.S. to World Court," *New York Times*, April 10, 1984 ("The Reagan Administration says Nicaragua is trying to overthrow the Salvadoran Government and that the mining of Nicaraguan harbors is therefore justified as a form of self-defense for El Salvador"); Outer Space Treaty (1967), in "Space Resource Mining—US Support for Commercial Exploitation," February 16, 2016, accessed July 26, 2016, http://interactive.satellitetoday.com /space-resource-mining-us-support-for-commercial-exploitation/; Elizabeth Shakman Hurd, *Beyond Religious Freedom* (Princeton, NJ: Princeton University Press, 2015).

8. "The Republic of Philippines v. the People's Republic of China," Permanent Court of Arbitration, accessed August 24, 2016, https://www.pcacases.com/web/view/7; President Barack Obama, "Remarks by the President in Address to the Nation on Syria," accessed August 24, 2016, https://www.whitehouse.gov/the-press-office /2013/09/10/remarks-president-address-nation-syria.

9. Tom Ginsburg and Tamir Moustafa, eds., *Rule by Law: The Politics of Courts in Authoritarian Regimes* (Cambridge: Cambridge University Press, 2008).

10. Samantha Besson, "The Authority of the Law: Lifting the State Veil," *Sydney Law Review* 31(2009): 343–80. See also Allen Buchanan, "The Legitimacy of International Law," in *The Philosophy of International Law*, ed. Samantha Besson and John Tasioulas (Oxford: Oxford University Press, 2010); Joseph Raz, *The Morality of Freedom* (Oxford: Clarendon Press, 1986); H.L.A. Hart, *Essays on Bentham* (Oxford: Oxford University Press, 1982).

11. This was part of the conversation between rationalism and constructivism as each sought to define its core commitments in distinction to the other. For a key statement on this, see Robert O. Keohane, "International Relations and International Law: Two Optics," *Harvard International Law Journal* 38, no. 2 (1997): 487–502.

12. As March and Olsen write, "On the one side are those who see action as driven by a logic of anticipated consequences and prior preferences. On the other side are those who see action as driven by a logic of appropriateness and a sense of identity." James G. March and Johan P. Olsen, "The Institutional Dynamics of International Political Orders," *International Organization* 52, no. 4 (1998): 949.

13. Oscar Schachter, "The Uses of Law in Peace-Keeping," *Virginia Law Review* 50, no. 6 (1964): 1099.

14. Pierre Bourdieu, "The Force of Law: Toward a Sociology of the Juridical Field," *Hastings Law Journal* 38, no. 5 (1987): 814–53.

15. Anthony Giddens, *The Consequences of Modernity* (Cambridge, UK: Polity, 1990); Zygmunt Bauman, *Liquid Modernity* (Cambridge, UK: Polity, 2000).

16. "Whaling in the Antarctic (Australia v. Japan: New Zealand Intervening)," ICJ, 2014, accessed August 24, 2016, http://www.icj-cij.org/docket/index.php?p1=3&p2=1&case=148&code=aj&p3=6.

17. Judith Shklar, *Legalism: Law, Morals, and Political Trials* (Cambridge, MA: Harvard University Press, 1964); Scott Veitch, *Law and Irresponsibility: On the Legitimation of Human Suffering* (Abingdon, UK: Routledge, 2007); Mara Pillinger, Ian Hurd, and Michael N. Barnett, "How to Get Away with Cholera: The UN, Haiti, and International Law," *Perspectives on Politics* 14, no. 1 (2016): 70–86. See also Philip Alston, "Report of the Special Rapporteur on Extreme Poverty and Human Rights," UN Office of the High Commissioner, 2016.

18. Helen Kinsella, *The Image before the Weapon: A Critical History of the Distinction between Combatant and Civilian* (Ithaca, NY: Cornell University Press, 2011). For the "life-and-death" stakes of legal interpretation, see Robert M. Cover, "Nomos and Narrative," *Harvard Law Review* 97 (1983–84): 4–68.

19. Bourdieu, *Outline of a Theory of Practice*; Behind Bourdieu, Taylor, Schatzki, and others are Ludwig Wittgenstein, Martin Heidegger, Max Weber, and many more.

20. Jutta Brunnée and Stephen J. Toope, "International Interactional Law: An Introduction," *International Theory* 3, no. 2 (2011): 27, 310.

21. On recursivity in international legal settings, see Terence C. Halliday, "Recursivity in Global Normmaking: A Sociolegal Agenda," *Law and Social Science* 5 (2009): 263–89.

22. Christian Reus-Smit, "Obligation through Practice," *International Theory* 3, no. 2 (2011): 342.

23. Charlotte Peevers, *The Politics of Justifying Force: The Suez Crisis, the Iraq War, and International Law* (Oxford: Oxford University Press, 2013), 30, 47.

24. Janina Dill, *Legitimate Targets? Social Construction, International Law, and US Bombing* (Cambridge: Cambridge University Press, 2015); Peevers, *The Politics of Justifying Force*; Adler and Pouliot, *International Practices*; Friedrich V. Kratochwil, *Rules, Norms, and Decisions: On the Conditions of Practical and Legal Reasoning in International Relations and Domestic Affairs* (Cambridge: Cambridge University Press, 1989).

25. Karl E. Weick, *Sensemaking in Organizations* (Thousand Oaks, CA: Sage, 1995), 3.

26. Charles Taylor, "To Follow a Rule . . . ," in *Bourdieu: Critical Perspectives*, ed.

Craig Calhoun, Edward LiPuma, and Moishe Postone (Chicago: University of Chicago Press, 1993), 45–60.

27. Frank I. Michelman, "Justification (and Justifiability) of Law in a Contradictory World," *Nomos* 28 (1986): 72. Emphasis in original

28. Neil MacCormick, "Argument and Interpretation in Law," *Argumentation* 6, no. 1 (1993): 19, cited in Scott Veitch, *Law and Irresponsibility: On the Legitimation of Human Suffering* (Abingdon, UK: Routledge-Cavendish, 2007), 77.

29. Scott Veitch, *Law and Irresponsibility: On the Legitimation of Human Suffering* (Abingdon, UK: Routledge, 2007), 76 (emphasis in original).

30. G. John Ikenberry, *After Victory: Institutions, Strategic Restraint, and the Rebuilding after Major War* (Princeton, NJ: Princeton University Press, 2001); Ruti G. Teitel, *Humanity's Law* (Oxford: Oxford University Press, 2013); Mary Ellen O'Connell, *The Power and Purpose of International Law: Insights from the Theory and Practice of Enforcement* (Oxford: Oxford University Press, 2008).

31. Martti Koskenniemi, *The Gentle Civilizer of Nations: The Rise and Fall of International Law, 1870–1960* (Cambridge: Cambridge University Press, 2004); Mark Mazower, *Governing the World: The History of an Idea, 1815 to the Present* (New York: Penguin, 2013); Benjamin Allen Coates, *Legalist Empire: International Law and American Foreign Relations in the Early Twentieth Century* (Oxford: Oxford University Press, 2016); Christian Reus-Smit, *The Moral Purpose of the State: Culture, Social Identity, and Institutional Rationality in International Relations* (Princeton, NJ: Princeton University Press, 1999); Brunnée and Toope, *Legitimacy and Legality in International Law.*

32. Jennifer Mitzen, *Power in Concert: The Nineteenth-Century Origins of Global Governance* (Chicago: University of Chicago Press, 2013).

33. On whether legal obligation "is best viewed as an internalized commitment [or] an externally imposed duty," see, versus the rationalists and others, Brunnée and Toope, *Legitimacy and Legality in International Law.*

34. Georg Sørensen, *A Liberal World Order in Crisis: Choosing between Imposition and Restraint* (Ithaca, NY: Cornell University Press, 2011), 141.

35. Beth A. Simmons, *Mobilizing for Human Rights: International Law in Domestic Politics* (Cambridge: Cambridge University Press, 2009), 7.

36. Arthur Watts, "The Importance of International Law," in *The Role of Law in International Politics*, ed. Michael Byers (Oxford: Oxford University Press, 2000), 5.

37. Ryan Goodman and Derek Jinks, for instance, open their study of the "effects of human rights treaties" with the question, "Does international law constrain state behaviour?" Ryan Goodman and Derek Jinks, "Measuring the Effects of Human Rights Treaties," *European Journal of International Law* 14, no. 1 (2003): 171.

38. Michael J. Glennon, "Why the Security Council Failed," *Foreign Affairs*, May–June 2003, accessed March 6, 2017, https://www.foreignaffairs.com/articles/iraq/2003-05-01/why-security-council-failed; Kenneth N. Waltz, "Structural Realism after the Cold War," *International Security* 25, no. 1 (2000): 5–41; Jack Goldsmith and Daryl Levinson, "Law for States: International Law, Constitutional Law, Public

Law," *Harvard Law Review* 122, no. 7 (2009): 1791–868; John J. Mearsheimer, *The Tragedy of Great Power Politics* (New York: W. W. Norton, 2001).

39. Beth Elize Whitaker, "Compliance among Weak States: Africa and the Counter-Terrorism Regime," *Review of International Studies* 36 (2010): 639–62; Andrew Guzman, *How International Law Works: A Rational Choice Theory* (Oxford: Oxford University Press, 2010); Chayes and Chayes, *The New Sovereignty*; Beth Simmons, "Compliance with International Agreements," *Annual Review of Political Science* 1 (1998): 75–93; Annyssa Bellal and Stuart Casey-Maslen, "Improving Compliance with International Law by Armed Non-State Actors," *Goettingen Journal of International Law* 3 (2001): 175–97; Robert O. Keohane, "Compliance with International Commitments: Politics within a Framework of Law," *Proceedings of the American Society of International Law* 86 (1992): 176–80.

40. With this litmus test in mind, it is clear that the difference between realists and liberals is not a disagreement about state interests (for instance, as absolute versus relative gains, or guns versus butter), or about the unit of analysis (state-centrism or a disaggregated state). It is instead a substantive disagreement about the empirical impact of international law and global governance on government decisions. Realists are those who strive to show that international law is not compelling to strong states, while liberals are those who strive to show that it sometimes is. On optimists and pessimists in this sense, see Laurence R. Helfer, "Monitoring Compliance with Unratified Treaties: The ILO Experience," *Law and Contemporary Problems* 71 (Winter 2008): 207. For a self-described pessimist view, see Joseph Grieco, "Anarchy and the Limits of Cooperation," *International Organization* 42, no. 3 (1988): 485–507. Ohlin describes realists as "skeptical that international law ever forces a state to change its behavior." Jens David Ohlin, *The Assault on International Law* (Oxford: Oxford University Press, 2015), 12. On compliance as the measure of rule strength, see Michael Glennon, "How International Rules Die," *Georgetown Law Journal* 93 (2005): 939–91.

41. David Kennedy, *A World of Struggle: How Power, Law, and Expertise Shape Global Political Economy* (Princeton, NJ: Princeton University Press, 2016), 240, cited in Samuel Moyn, "Knowledge and Politics in International Law," *Harvard Law Review* 129 (2016): 2176.

Chapter 4: The Permissive Power of the Ban on War

1. Michael Byers, *War Law: Understanding International Law in Armed Conflict* (New York: Grove Press, 2005), 148. See also Mary Ellen O'Connell, "War and Peace," in *The Oxford Handbook of the History of International Law*, ed. Bardo Fassbender and Anne Peters (Oxford: Oxford University Press, 2012).

2. See, for instance, G. John Ikenberry and Anne-Marie Slaughter, *Forging a World of Liberty under Law: U.S. National Security in the 21st Century* (Princeton, NJ: Woodrow Wilson School, 2006), accessed March 6, 2017, http://www.princeton.edu/~ppns/report/FinalReport.pdf.

3. Helen M. Kinsella, *The Image before the Weapon: A Critical History of the Distinction between Combatant and Civilian* (Ithaca, NY: Cornell University Press, 2011); Bernard Harcourt, *The Illusion of Free Markets: Punishment and the Myth of Natural Order* (Cambridge, MA: Harvard University Press, 2012).

4. On this, see Shirley V. Scott, *International Law, US Power: The United States' Quest for Legal Security* (Cambridge: Cambridge University Press, 2012); Oscar Schachter, "The Legality of Pro-Democratic Intervention," *American Journal of International Law* 78 (1984): 648.

5. Ian Hurd, *After Anarchy: Power and Legitimacy in the UN Security Council* (Princeton, NJ: Princeton University Press, 2007).

6. The Kellogg-Briand Pact (also known as the Pact of Paris, and more formally as the General Treaty for the Renunciation of War as an Instrument of National Policy) was for a time the most widely ratified international instrument. It bans war by its parties in their relations among each other, but leaves unaffected their wars with others. The treaty has just two operative paragraphs, which require that parties "condemn the recourse to war for the solution of international controversies, and renounce it as an instrument of national policy in their relations with one another" (Article I), and "agree that the settlement or solution of all disputes or conflicts, of whatever nature or of whatever origin they may be, which may arise among them, shall never be sought except by pacific means" (Article II). It remains in effect today among its signatories.

7. See the discussion in Stanimir A. Alexandrov, *Self-Defense against the Use of Force in International Law* (Dordrecht: Kluwer, 1996).

8. The recent wave of scholarly interest at the boundary between political science and legal studies on the "legalization" of world politics has not addressed this case. See, for instance, Judith L. Goldstein, Miles Kahler, Robert O. Keohane, and Anne-Marie Slaughter, eds., *Legalization and World Politics* (Cambridge, MA: MIT Press, 2001); Jeffrey L. Dunoff and Mark A. Pollack, eds., *Interdisciplinary Perspectives on International Law and International Relations: The State of the Art* (New York: Cambridge University Press, 2013); Terence C. Halliday and Gregory Shaffer, eds., *Transnational Legal Orders* (New York: Cambridge University Press, 2015). See also Oona A. Hathaway and Scott Shapiro, *The Worst Crime of All* (New York: Simon and Schuster, 2017).

9. Tom Ruys, *'Armed Attack' and Article 51 of the UN Charter: Evolutions in Customary Law and Practice* (Cambridge: Cambridge University Press, 2010), 11.

10. Hathaway and Shapiro, *The Worst Crime of All.*

11. Martha Finnemore, *The Purpose of Intervention: Changing Beliefs about the Use of Force* (Ithaca, NY: Cornell University Press, 2004).

12. Byers, *War Law*; Hathaway and Shapiro, *The Worst Crime of All.* See also the account of European "stability" governed by the Concert of Europe in Jennifer Mitzen, *Power in Concert: The Nineteenth-Century Origins of Global Governance* (Chicago: University of Chicago Press, 2013).

13. Christine Gray, *International Law and the Use of Force*, 3rd ed. (Oxford: Oxford University Press, 2008), 6.

14. Michael Byers, "Jumping the Gun," *London Review of Books* 24, no. 14 (2002): 3–5.

15. Thomas M. Franck, *Recourse to Force: State Action against Threats and Armed Attacks* (Cambridge: Cambridge University Press, 2002), 10.

16. The naive version assumes that changing the law will necessarily change behavior accordingly. This is a straw target, easier to caricature than to actually find in scholarship. For the original statement of world peace through law, see Grenville Clark and Louis B. Sohn, *World Peace through World Law* (Cambridge, MA: Harvard University Press, 1958). For a debunking of the myth of legal naïveté in relation to the 1928 Kellogg-Briand Pact, see Harold Josephson, "Outlawing War: Internationalism and the Pact of Paris," *Diplomatic History* 3, no. 4 (1999): 377–90.

17. Hedley Bull, *The Anarchical Society: A Study in World Order*, 3rd ed. (New York: Columbia University Press, 2002).

18. Hersch Lauterpacht, *The Function of Law in the International Community* (1933), 64, cited in Franck, *Recourse to Force*, 1.

19. O'Connell, "War and Peace,"272. As Rosa Brooks says, "At its most fundamental level, the rule of law is concerned with constraining and ordering power and violence." Rosa Brooks, "Drones and the International Rule of Law," *Ethics and International Affairs* 28, no. 1 (2014): 83.

20. Compare this to, for instance, Leo Strauss, who suggests "the broader consideration of what law is for, namely the existence, preferably on a high level, of political society as a whole," not just the regulation of violence. Leo Strauss, "Seminar on the Philosophy of History," cited in Robert Howse, *Leo Strauss: Man of Peace* (New York: Cambridge University Press, 2014), 130.

21. G. John Ikenberry, *Liberal Leviathan: The Origins, Crisis, and Transformation of the American World Order* (Princeton, NJ: Princeton University Press, 2011), 106.

22. Ibid., 18. See also Stephen G. Brooks and William C. Wohlforth, *America Abroad: The United States' Global Role in the 21st Century* (Oxford: Oxford University Press, 2016).

23. Ikenberry, *Liberal Leviathan*, 84.

24. Ibid.

25. Henry R. Nau, *Conservative Internationalism: Armed Diplomacy under Jefferson, Polk, Truman, and Reagan* (Princeton, NJ: Princeton University Press, 2014), 228. He identifies Iran as a "threat" to world order because it exhibits "less respect for international rules" than does the United States (231). Nau also says that the US "failure" to use the collective self-defense provisions of the North Atlantic Treaty Organization charter (Art. V) was a mistake of historic proportions, "one of the great mysteries and tragedies of the history of 9/11" (237).

26. Ibid., 232.

27. Michael Hardt and Antonio Negri, *Empire* (Cambridge, MA: Harvard University Press, 2000), 14. See also Hauke Brunkhorst, *Critical Theory of Legal Revolutions: Evolutionary Perspectives* (London: Bloomsbury, 2014), esp. 3.IV.

28. B. S. Chimni, "International Institutions Today: An Imperial Global State in the Making," *European Journal of International Law* 15, no. 1 (2004): 1–37.

29. Hardt and Negri, *Empire*, 18, 15.

30. Mitzen, *Power in Concert*; Paul Sharp, *Diplomatic Theory of International Relations* (Cambridge: Cambridge University Press, 2009).

31. See, for instance, Andrew Guzman, *How International Law Works: A Rational Choice Theory* (Oxford: Oxford University Press, 2010).

32. This is based in part on the hierarchy of legal sources set out in Article 38(1) of the Statute of the ICJ, and in part on customary law and state practice. See Christopher Greenwood, "The Sources of International Law: An Introduction," accessed March 7, 2017, http://legal.un.org/avl/pdf/ls/greenwood_outline.pdf. Several book-length treatments exist including Gray, *International Law and the Use of Force*; Franck, *Recourse to Force*; Mary Ellen O'Connell, *The Power and Purpose of International Law: Insights from the Theory and Practice of Enforcement* (Oxford: Oxford University Press, 2008). On self-defense in particular, see Stanimir A. Alexandrov, *Self-Defense against the Use of Force in International Law* (Leiden: Martinus Nijhoff, 1996), chap. 17.

33. This is set out in the Vienna Convention on the Law of Treaties (1969) in Article 31(1).

34. See *Yearbook of the United Nations* (New York: Department of Public Information, 1982), 1319–47.

35. UN Resolution 661, accessed March 9, 2017, https://documents-dds-ny.un.org/doc/RESOLUTION/GEN/NR0/575/11/IMG/NR057511.pdf?OpenElement.

36. For contestation over this among US legal scholars, see "Agora: Future Implications of the Iraq Conflict," *American Journal of International Law* 93 (2003).

37. For a rare exception, see Byers, "Jumping the Gun," 5: "The UN Charter provides a clear answer to these questions: in the absence of an armed attack, the Security Council alone can act." This is at odd with Byers in *War Law*, reflecting perhaps the fact that for Byers, the US invasion of Iraq was not the sort of war that should be legitimated by finding it to be legal under the Charter.

38. See, for instance, Ruys, *'Armed Attack' and Article 51 of the UN Charter*, chap. 1; Olivier Corten, "The Controversies over the Customary Prohibition on the Use of Force: A Methodological Debate," *European Journal of International Law* 16, no. 5 (2006): 803–22; Duncan B. Hollis, "The Existential Function of Interpretation in International Law," Temple University Legal Studies Research Paper Series, 2013–43, 2013; Ingo Venzke, "Is Interpretation in International Law a Game?" in *Interpretation in International Law*, ed. Andrea Bianchi, Daniel Peat, and Matthew Windsor (Oxford: Oxford University Press, 2014), 352–69; Alexander Orakhelashvili, *The Interpretation of Acts and Rules in Public International Law* (Oxford: Oxford University Press 2008); Duncan B. Hollis, ed., *The Oxford Guide to Treaties* (Oxford: Oxford University Press, 2012).

39. Franck, *Recourse to Force*, 51.

40. On legal interpretation, see Orakhelashvili, *The Interpretation of Acts and Rules in Public International Law*; Ingo Venzke, *How Interpretation Makes International Law* (Oxford: Oxford University Press, 2012); Hollis, "The Existential Function of International Law." See also Katharina Berner, "Authentic Interpretation in Public International Law" (paper presented to the Rule of Law Center, WZB, 2014). As Hollis says

"International law does not exist without interpretation" (1). See also Chimène I. Keitner, "'Cheap Talk' about Customary Law," in *International Law and the U.S. Supreme Court*, ed. David L. Sloss, Michael D. Ramsay, and William S. Dodge (Cambridge: Cambridge University Press, 2011), 494–98.

41. See the references in Oscar Schachter, "Self-Defense and the Rule of Law," *American Journal of International Law* 83 (1989): 263n22. See also Franck, *Recourse to Force*, 50. In both the Iraq-Kuwait War in 1990 and the Afghanistan War in 2001, for instance, the states invoking self-defense did not defer to the Council and the Council followed up by affirming their right not to do so.

42. Among others, Ikenberry in *Liberal Leviathan* (259) observes, "The notion that states have a right of self-defense in the face of an 'imminent threat' was widely recognized in international law and diplomacy." The consensus around this even includes scholars who are otherwise committed to a literal reading of the Charter. Schachter, as an example, is generally opposed to "expanded conceptions of self-defense," but he finds it unproblematic to say that there is "strong resistance to widening self-defense to permit force except where there has been an armed attack or threat of armed attack." By accepting the legality of anticipatory self-defense, he is accepting the "expanded" conception and arguing in effect that it should not be expanded any further. Schachter, "Self-Defense and the Rule of Law," 271, 273.

43. Variations, of course, exist. The idea of "imminence" is often derived from Daniel Webster, who said that anticipatory acts are acceptable when "the necessity of that self-defense is instant, overwhelming, and leaving no choice of means, and no moment of deliberation." Daniel Webster, "Letter to Henry Stephen Fox," in *The Papers of Daniel Webster: Diplomatic Papers, vol. I, 1841–1843*, ed. Kenneth E. Shewmaker (Lebanon, NH: Dartmouth College Press, 1983).

44. The issue of "anticipation" came up in 1945 and was struck down by the Five Powers that dominated the Charter-drafting process. The United States considered the issue internally in its delegation, and Harold Stassen expressed the definitive official position against it: "This was intentional. . . . [W]e did not want exercised the right of self-defense before an armed attack had occurred." Ruys, *'Armed Attack' and Article 51 of the UN Charter*, 65, citing Ralph R. Goodwin, Herbert A. Fine, Velma H. Cassidy, and Francis C. Prescott, eds., *Foreign Relations of the United States (1945)* (Washington, DC: US Government Printing Office, 1969), 818.

45. It is in fact integral to treaty interpretation in international law. See Georg Nolte, ed., *Treaties and Subsequent Practice* (Oxford: Oxford University Press, 2013).

46. Franck, *Recourse to Force*, 21.

47. W. Michael Reisman, "Coercion and Self-Determination: Construing Article 2(4)," *American Journal of International Law* 78 (1984): 644–45.

48. Ruys, *'Armed Attack' and Article 51 of the UN Charter*, 511; Franck, *Recourse to Force*, 21.

49. Byers, *War Law*, 60.

50. Ruys, *'Armed Attack' and Article 51 of the UN Charter*, 6. It is through this process that many states and scholars have contended that humanitarian intervention has become a legal form of international military action. As states have come to see

humanitarian intervention as desirable, they have consequently asserted that it is legal under the Charter. Belgium made this argument at the ICJ in the Legality of the Use of Force case, as did the United Kingdom in relation to the Kosovo bombing: "The action being taken is legal. It is justified as an exceptional measure to prevent an overwhelming humanitarian catastrophe. . . . In these circumstances, military intervention is legally justifiable." (Gray, *International Law and the Use of Force*, 42).

51. Franck, *Recourse to Force*, 49.

52. Reisman, "Coercion and Self-Determination," 644.

53. Jan Klabbers, cited in Ramses Wessel, "Executive Boards and Councils," in *The Oxford Handbook of International Organizations*, ed. Jacob Katz Cogan, Ian Hurd, and Ian Johnstone (Oxford: Oxford University Press, 2016), 802–21.

54. On the uses of history, see Sam Moyn, *Human Rights and the Uses of History* (London: Verso, 2014).

55. Schachter, "Self-Defense and the Rule of Law," 268.

56. The phrase comes from Strauss's discussion of Thucydides in Robert Howse, *Leo Strauss: Man of Peace* (New York Cambridge University Press, 2014), 135.

57. "Military and Paramilitary Activities in and against Nicaragua (Nicaragua v. United States of America," ICJ, accessed March 9, 2017, http://www.icj-cij.org/docket /index.php?sum=367&code=nus&p1=3&p2=3&case=70&k=66&p3=5.

58. This mirrors a shift in realist thinking about IR from a "balance against power" model to a "balance against threat" model, following Stephen M. Walt, "Alliance Formation and the Balance of World Power," *International Security* 9, no. 4 (Spring 1985): 3–43.

59. On Entebbe, see the debate between Jeffrey Sheenan and Jordan Paust. Jeffrey A. Sheehan, "The Entebbe Raid: The Principle of Self-Help in International Law as Justification for State Use of Armed Force," *Fletcher Forum of World Affairs* 1 (1977): 135–53; Jordan J. Paust, "Entebbe and Self-Help: The Israeli Response to Terrorism," *Fletcher Forum of World Affairs* 2, no. 1 (1978): 86–93. On military action on behalf of citizens abroad, see Ruys, *'Armed Attack' and Article 51 of the UN Charter*.

60. US Department of Justice, "Attorney General Eric Holder Speaks at Northwestern University Law School," March 5, 2012, accessed March 9, 2017, http://www .justice.gov/iso/opa/ag/speeches/2012/ag-speech-1203051.html.

61. Alexandrov *Self-Defense against the Use of Force in International Law*, chap. 17. See also the justification of US military action against "sharp local deviations" from US preferences in South American governments in Oscar Schachter, *Toward Wider Acceptance of UN Treaties* (New York: Arno Press, 1971), 546.

62. North Atlantic Treaty Organization, "NATO Ten Years After: Learning the Lessons," September 11, 2011, accessed March 9, 2017, http://www.nato.int/docu /review/2011/11-september/10-years-sept-11/EN/index.htm.

63. Kinsella, *The Image before the Weapon*.

64. Consider a passage from Louis Henkin, as he argued in that Article 2(4) had been influential in shaping US foreign policy: "Few believe that the OAS [Organization of American States] or even the United States alone would use force against the political independence or territorial integrity of any country in the

[Western] Hemisphere, even in the event of sharp local deviation, if it was not in fact abetted from the outside." Henkin meant this to show how profoundly the ban on war had come to be taken for granted in US foreign policy, and his belief that it would be violated only in extreme circumstances, although imagining that such extreme circumstances would be satisfied if unwelcome behaviors of foreign governments were a result of involved outside influence. Thus, for Henkin, Article 2(4) did not prohibit the use of force by the United States in Latin America if it was a response to Soviet or other "outside" actions there. Louis Henkin, "Reports of the Death of Article 2(4) Are Greatly Exaggerated," *American Journal of International Law* 65 (1971): 546.

65. The US attack on Libya in 1986 was characterized as "self-defense" by the United States but came a full ten days after the bombing of a Berlin disco that apparently provoked it.

66. Anthony D'Amato says self-defense is "a loophole that gets wider the more one looks at it." Anthony D'Amato, "The Invasion of Panama Was a Lawful Response to Tyranny," *American Journal of International Law* 84 (1990): 516–24.

67. On the first, see Guzman, *How International Law Works*. On the second, see Oona A. Hathaway, "Do Human Rights Treaties Make a Difference?" Faculty Scholarship Series Paper 839, 2002, accessed March 9, 2017, http://digitalcommons.law.yale.edu/cgi/viewcontent.cgi?article=1852&context=fss_papers.

68. Joseph Raz, "Reasons: Practical and Adaptive," in *Reasons for Action*, ed. David Sobel and Steven Wall (Cambridge: Cambridge University Press, 2011), 37–57.

69. On prodemocracy intervention, see D'Amato, "The Invasion of Panama Was a Lawful Response to Tyranny." On humanitarian intervention, see Franck, *Recourse to Force*. On the responsibility to protect, see Gareth Evans and Mohamed Sahnoun, "The Responsibility to Protect," *Foreign Affairs* 81, no. 6 (2002), accessed March 9, 2017, https://www.foreignaffairs.com/articles/2002-11-01/responsibility-protect.

70. See, for instance, Charles Taylor, "To Follow a Rule . . . ," in *Bourdieu: Critical Perspectives*, ed. Craig Calhoun, Edward LiPuma, and Moishe Postone (Chicago: University of Chicago Press, 1993), 45–60.

71. Finnemore, *The Purpose of Intervention*.

72. Kenneth N. Waltz, *Theory of International Politics* (Hoboken, NJ: Wiley, 1979).

73. Thomas M. Franck, "Who Killed Article 2(4)? or: Changing Norms Governing the Use of Force by States," *American Journal of International Law* 64 (1970): 809–37; Michael Glennon, "The Fog of Law: Self-Defense, Inherence, and Incoherence in Article 51 of the United Nations Charter," *Harvard Journal of Law and Public Policy* 25 (2001): 539–58.

74. Cited in O'Connell, "War and Peace," 275.

75. Karl Marx, "For a Ruthless Criticism of Everything Existing" (also known as "Letter from Marx to Arnold Ruge"), in *The Marx-Engels Reader*, ed. Robert C. Tucker, 2nd ed. (New York: W. W. Norton, 1978), 15.

76. Reisman, "Coercion and Self-Determination," 643.

77. Ruys, *'Armed Attack' and Article 51 of the UN Charter*, 4.

78. Byers, *War Law*, 155. See also the ICJ Nicaragua expectation that "the conduct of States should, in general, be consistent with such rules" rather than that "the application of the rules in question should have been perfect." Nicaragua case, para. 186, cited in Gray, *International Law and the Use of Force*, 25

Chapter 5: The Rule of No Law

1. For a discussion of various ways that gaps in international law might be approached and the implications for the separation of politics from law in world affairs, see Martti Koskenniemi, "Introduction," in *The Function of Law in the International Community*, ed. Hersch Lauterpacht (Oxford: Oxford University Press, 2011), xxix–xlvii. Jean D'Aspremont sets out the terms of the debate, and advances a practice-based approach to figuring out what legal rules say as well as distinguishing between legal and nonlegal resources. Jean D'Aspremont, *Formalism and International Law: A Theory of the Ascertainment of Legal Rules* (Oxford: Oxford University Press, 2011).

2. Judith Goldstein, Miles Kahler, Robert O. Keohane, and Anne-Marie Slaughter, "Introduction: Legalization and World Politics," *International Organization* 54, no. 3 (2000): 391; Terence C. Halliday and Gregory Shaffer, "Transnational Legal Orders," in *Transnational Legal Orders*, ed. Terence C. Halliday and Gregory Shaffer (New York: Cambridge University Press, 2015), 7.

3. This was in the context of a request by the UN General Assembly for an advisory opinion on the question. These are nonbinding opinions on questions of law that carry some weight in legal and political disputes given the legitimacy of the ICJ on international legal issues.

4. "Legality of the Threat or Use of Nuclear Weapons," accessed March 9, 2017, http://www.icj-cij.org/docket/files/95/7495.pdf, 2, 261.

5. On the regulation of non liquet at tribunals, see Hersch Lauterpacht, "Some Observations on the Prohibition of 'Non Liquet' and the Completeness of International Law," in *International Law Collected Papers*, ed. Eli Lauterpacht and Hersch Lauterpacht, vol. 2 (Cambridge University Press, 1975), 2:213–37. In contrast, see Julius Stone, "Non-Liquet and the Function of Law in the International Community," *British Year Book of International Law* 35 (1959): 124–47; Prosper Weil, " 'The Court Cannot Conclude Definitively . . .': Non Liquet Revisited," *Columbia Journal of Transnational Law* 36 (1998): 109–19; Amos O. Enabulele, "The Avoidance of Non Liquet by the International Court of Justice, the Completeness of the Sources of International Law in Article 38(1) of the Statute of the Court, and the Role of Judicial Decisions in Article 38(1)(d)," *Commonwealth Law Bulletin* 38, no. 4 (2012): 617–52.

6. Mariano J. Aznar-Gomez, "The 1996 Nuclear Weapons Advisory Opinion and Non Liquet in International Law," *International and Comparative Law Quarterly* 48, no. 1 (January 1999): 15.

7. Ilmar Tammelo, "On the Logical Openness of Legal Systems: A Modal Analysis of Law with Special Reference to the Logical Status of Non Liquet in International Law," *American Journal of Comparative Law 1959* 8, no. 2 (Spring 1959): 187–203.

8. See, for instance, Mia Swart, "Gap-Filling as Law-Making: The Examples of the Ad Hoc Criminal Tribunals," in *Select Proceedings of the European Society of International Law*, ed. Hélène Ruiz Fabri, Rüdiger Wolfrum, and Jana Goldin (London: Hart Publishing, 2008).

9. Weiss notes that the Lotus case was decided by a "majority" of six judges out of twelve, with the presiding judge casting the deciding vote. Peter Weiss, "The World Court Tackles the Fate of the Earth: An Introduction to the ICJ Advisory Opinion on the Legality of the Threat and Use of Nuclear Weapons," *Translational Law and Contemporary Problems* 313 (1997): 320n21.

10. *The Case of the S.S. Lotus*, Permanent Court of International Justice 1927.

11. N. Papadakis, *The International Legal Regime of Artificial Islands* (Heidelberg: Springer, 1977): 129, citing a Dutch claim in the 1960s that relies on the work of J.P.A. François on the legal vacuum.

12. John R. Bolton, "Is There Really a 'Law' of International Affairs?" *Transnational Law and Contemporary Problems* 10 (2000): 2.

13. Jens David Ohlin, *The Assault on International Law* (Ithaca, NY: Cornell University Press, 2015), 87.

14. ICJ Report 1996, 291, para. 9. They may be constrained in how or when they are used if laws exist on these issues, as I discuss below.

15. ICJ Haya de la Torre case, cited in Prosper Weil, "The Court Cannot Conclude Definitively," 113.

16. The wording is slightly different elsewhere in the opinion, where it is said that legality depends on the "self-defense of a state" being at stake. The subtle difference between these two wordings produces a debate over whether it is the nuclear user's self-defense or that of any of its allies that matters for legality.

17. Isabel Hull, *A Scrap of Paper: Breaking and Making International Law in the First World War* (Ithaca, NY: Cornell University Press, 2014). For a discussion of the productive power of military technology on what might be called social, legal, and political forms, see Carl Schmitt, *The Nomos of the Earth in the International Law of the Jus Publicum Europeaum, 2003/1950* (Candor, NY: Telos Press), part 4, chap. 7.

18. It is easy to imagine what such a treaty might look like, modeled perhaps on treaties that regulate other weapons such as land mines, chemical weapons, and space-based weapons. Many activist groups have advanced draft treaties to regulate drones. See, for instance, "Statement on the Use of Unmanned Armed Aerial Vehicles," accessed December 4, 2015, http://www.space4peace.org/uav/gn_statement_on_drones.htm.

19. In theory, see Eric A. Posner and Jack L. Goldsmith, "Moral and Legal Rhetoric in International Relations: A Rational Choice Perspective," John M. Olin Program in Law and Economics Working Paper Series, no. 108, 2000. In practice, see Anu Bradford and Eric A. Posner, "Universal Exceptionalism in International Law," *Harvard International Law Journal* 52, no. 11 (2011): 1–54.

20. I focus on the position of the US government here, conscious that the position is in part constituted by arguments made by individuals in various capacities, official and private, American and otherwise. On the separation of the two arguments, see

Michael W. Lewis and Vincent J. Vitkowsky, "The Use of Drones and Targeted Killing in Counterterrorism," *Engage* 12, no. 1 (2011): 73–76.

21. Harold Koh, "The Obama Administration and International Law" (address to the American Society of International Law annual meeting, 2010).

22. Ibid.

23. I am interested here in the legal politics of drones, and so do not take up the debate over whether they are counterproductive to the stated goals of the United States or other users. On this, see Audrey Kurth Cronin, "Why Drones Fail: When Tactics Drive Strategy," *Foreign Affairs* 92 (2013), accessed March 9, 2017, https://www.foreignaffairs.com/articles/somalia/2013-06-11/why-drones-fail. Ryan Vogel says the practice has been "spectacularly successful" at killing targets cheaply, though perhaps not in any broader sense. Ryan J. Vogel, "Drone Warfare and the Law of Armed Conflict," *Denver Journal of International Law and Policy* 39, no. 1 (2010): 102.

24. Philip Alston, "Study on Targeted Killings," Report of the Special Rapporteur on Extrajudicial, Summary, or Arbitrary Executions, United Nations A/HRC/14/24/Add.6, May 28, 2010.

25. Micah Zenko, "The United States Doesn't Know Who It's Killing," foreignpolicy.com, April 23, 2015, accessed September 29, 2016, http://www.cfr.org/drones/united-states-does-not-know-s-killing/p36472.

26. On the legal obligation to try to capture enemies, see Mary Ellen O'Connell, "To Kill or Capture Suspects in the Global War on Terror," *Case Western Reserve Journal of International Law* 35 (2003): 325–32. On due process in US law, see Benjamin McKelvey, "Due Process Rights and the Targeted Killing of Suspected Terrorists: The Unconstitutional Scope of Executive Killing Power," *Vanderbilt Journal of Transnational Law* 44, no. 5 (2011): 1353–66.

27. Christoph Heyns, "Report of the Special Rapporteur on Extrajudicial, Summary, or Arbitrary Executions," UN A/68/382, para. 29.

28. Amnesty International "Killing Outside the Bounds of Law," accessed January 6, 2015, http://www.amnestyusa.org/our-work/issues/security-and-human-rights/drones. Mary Ellen O'Connell disagrees with the war frame and concludes that civilian deaths are too high to justify under nonwar legal frames. Mary Ellen O'Connell, "Lawful Use of Combat Drones," Testimony to the Subcommittee on National Security and Foreign Affairs, US House of Representatives, April 28, 2010, accessed April 14, 2017, https://fas.org/irp/congress/2010_hr/042810oconnell.pdf. UN Special Rapporteur Heyns sees drones practice as a change from and threat to post-1945 legal order.

29. See, for instance, Obama's Speech on Drone Policy," May 23, 2013, accessed March 9, 2017, http://www.nytimes.com/2013/05/24/us/politics/transcript-of-obamas-speech-on-drone-policy.html; Koh, "The Obama Administration and International Law"; Eric Holder speech at Northwestern Law School, March 5, 2012.

30. See, for instance, Chris Jenks, "Law from Above: Unmanned Aerial Systems, Use of Force, and the Law of Armed Conflict," *North Dakota Law Review* 85 (2009): 649–71.

31. Charlie Savage, *Power Wars: Inside Obama's Post-9/11 Presidency* (Boston: Little, Brown and Company, 2015), 60.

32. Hague Convention on the Opening of Hostilities, Art. 1, 1907.

33. See Mary Ellen O'Connell, "Defining Armed Conflict," *Journal of Conflict and Security Law* 13 (2008): 393–400.

34. Vogel says that "the primary legal framework applicable to drone attacks conducted in the current conflict is the lex specialis of armed conflict." Vogel, "Drone Warfare and the Law of Armed Conflict," 113.

35. Authorization to Use Military Force, P.L. 107–40. Rosa Brooks calls this "the functional equivalent of a declaration of war." Rosa Brooks, "Cross-Border Targeted Killings: 'Lawful but Awful?'" *Harvard Journal of Law and Public Policy* 38 (2014): 237.

36. Koh, "The Obama Administration and International Law." See also Milena Sterio, "The United States' Use of Drones in the War on Terror: The (Il)legality of Targeted Killings under International Law," *Case Western Reserve Journal of International Law* 45 (2012): 201–4.

37. See, for instance, the US Supreme Court in Hamdan.

38. Vogel, "Drone Warfare and the Law of Armed Conflict," 107.

39. White House, Office of the Press Secretary, "Fact Sheet: The President's May 23 Speech on Counterterrorism," May 23, 2010, accessed March 9, 2017, https://www .whitehouse.gov/the-press-office/2013/05/23/fact-sheet-president-s-may-23-speech -counterterrorism. The 9/11 Commission took the view that "killing a person who posed an imminent threat to the United States would be an act of self-defense, not an assassination" Cited in Savage, *Power Wars.*

40. Sterio, "The United States' Use of Drones in the War on Terror."

41. For a similar pattern over US detention practices, see Ingo Venzke, "Legal Contestation about 'Enemy Combatants': On the Exercise of Power in Legal Interpretation," *Journal of International Law and International Relations* 5, no. 1 (2009): 155–84. I am setting aside nonlegal complaints, including that the political effects of drones undermines the stated goals of US policy. See, for instance, Brooks, "Cross-Border Targeted Killings."

42. See, for instance, John R. Bolton, "Is There Really a 'Law' of International Affairs?" *Transnational Law and Contemporary Problems* 10 (2000): 1-48.

43. David Kennedy, *Of War and Law* (Princeton, NJ: Princeton University Press, 2006).

44. See also Helen Kinsella, *The Image before the Weapon: A Critical History of the Distinction between Combatant and Civilian* (Ithaca, NY: Cornell University Press, 2011).

45. Michael Shank and Elizabeth Beavers, "Sign a Drone Treaty before Everyone Does as We Do," USNews.com, February 2, 2014, accessed March 9, 2017, http://www .usnews.com/opinion/blogs/world-report/2014/02/04/us-must-support-an-interna tional-drone-treaty; Campaign to Stop Killer Robots, accessed March 9, 2017, https:// www.stopkillerrobots.org; Louise Arimatsu, "A Treaty for Governing Cyber-

Weapons: Potential Benefits and Practical Limitations," fourth International Conference on Cyber Conflict, North Atlantic Treaty Organization Cooperative Cyber Defense Centre of Excellence, 2012, accessed March 9, 2017, https://ccdcoe.org/cycon/2012/proceedings/d3r1s6_arimatsu.pdf.

46. Jan Klabbers, "Reluctant Grundnormen: Articles 31(3)(c) and 42 of the Vienna Convention on the Law of Treaties and the Fragmentation of International Law," in *Time, History, and International Law*, ed., Matthew Craven, Malgosia Fitzmaurice, and Maria Vogiatzi (Leiden: Brill, 2007), 141, cited in Andrea Bianchi, "The Game of Interpretation in International Law: The Players, the Cards, and Why the Game Is Worth the Candle," in *Interpretation in International Law*, ed. Andrea Bianchi, Daniel Peat, and Matthew Windsor (Oxford: Oxford University Press, 2015), 55.

47. Goldstein, Kahler, Keohane, and Slaughter, "Introduction: Legalization and World Politics," 386.

48. Bonnie Honig, *Political Theory and the Displacement of Politics* (Ithaca, NY: Cornell University Press, 1993); Scott Veitch, *Law and Irresponsibility: On the Legitimation of Human Suffering* (Abingdon, UK: Routledge-Cavendish, 2007); Judith Shklar, *Legalism: Law, Morals, and Political Trials* (Cambridge, MA: Harvard University Press, 1986), 1.

49. Honig, *Political Theory and the Displacement of Politics*, 2.

50. Fuad Zarbiyev, "A Genealogy of Textualism in Treaty Interpretation," in *Interpretation in International Law*, ed. Andrea Bianchi, Daniel Peat, and Matthew Windsor (Oxford: Oxford University Press, 2015), 259.

51. Shklar, *Legalism*, 34.

52. On the politics of interpretation in international law, with an eye on a critical theory of interpretation itself and the "performative dimension and political consequences of interpretive speech acts," see Jens Olesen, "Toward a Politics of Hermeneutics," in *Interpretation in International Law*, ed. Andrea Bianchi, Daniel Peat, and Matthew Windsor (Oxford: Oxford University Press, 2015), 313.

53. Martti Koskenniemi, *From Apology to Utopia: The Structure of Legal Argument* (Cambridge: Cambridge University Press, 2005), viii.

Chapter 6: Torture

1. Beth A. Simmons and Allison Danner, "Credible Commitments and the International Criminal Court," *International Organization* 64 (2010): 225–56; James D. Morrow, "The Institutional Features of the Prisoners of War Treaties," *International Organization* 55, no. 4 (2001): 971–91; Barbara Koremenos, *The Continent of International Law* (Cambridge: Cambridge University Press, 2016); Ruti G. Teitel, *Humanity's Law* (Oxford: Oxford University Press, 2011); Leslie Johns, *Strengthening International Courts: The Hidden Costs of Legalization* (Ann Arbor: University of Michigan Press, 2015); Karen J. Alter, *The New Terrain of International Courts: Courts, Politics, Rights* (Princeton, NJ: Princeton University Press, 2014); Samuel P. Baumgartner, "Does Access to Justice Improve Countries' Compliance with Human Rights Norms?—An

Empirical Study," *Cornell International Law Journal* 44 (2011): 441–91; Courtney Hillebrecht, ed., *Domestic Politics and International Human Rights Tribunals* (New York; Cambridge University Press, 2014); Ryan Goodman and Derek Jinks, "Incomplete Internalization and Compliance with Human Rights Law," *European Journal of International Law* 19, no. 4 (2008): 725–48; Andreas Føllesdal, Johan Karlsson Schaffer, and Geir Ulfstein, eds., *The Legitimacy of International Human Rights Regimes: Legal, Political, and Philosophical Perspectives* (Cambridge: Cambridge University Press, 2014); Margaret E. Keck and Kathryn Sikkink, *Activists beyond Borders: Advocacy Networks in International Politics* (Ithaca, NY: Cornell University Press, 1998); Beth A. Simmons, *Mobilizing for Human Rights: International Law in Domestic Politics* (Cambridge: Cambridge University Press, 2009).

2. Emilie M. Hafner-Burton, David G. Victor, and Yonatan Lupu, "Political Science Research on International Law: The State of the Field," *American Journal of International Law* 106, no. 1 (2012): 47–97; Gregory Shaffer and Tom Ginsburg, "The Empirical Turn in International Legal Scholarship," *American Journal of International Law* 106, no. 1 (2012): 1–46; Jeffrey L. Dunoff and Mark A. Pollack, eds., *Interdisciplinary Perspectives on International Law and International Relations: The State of the Art* (New York: Cambridge University Press, 2012). Alexander Betts and Phil Orchard also consider how "norm implementation" affects compliance, giving a constructivist background to the compliance approach. Alexander Betts and Phil Orchard, eds., introduction to *Implementation and World Politics: How International Norms Change Practice* (Oxford: Oxford University Press, 2014). On the compliance gap at the heart of international law and organization, see Edward C. Luck and Michael W. Doyle, eds., *International Law and Organization: Closing the Compliance Gap* (Lanham, MD: Rowman and Littlefield, 2004).

3. For a classical statement on this distinction that posits norm following as an alternative to interest following, see Robert O. Keohane, "International Relations and International Law: Two Optics," *Harvard International Law Journal* 38, no. 2 (1997): 487–502. The same instinct to separate interests and norms as motivations for action underlies James G. March and Johan P. Olsen, "The Logic of Appropriateness," in *Oxford Handbook of Public Policy*, ed. Michael Moran, Martin Rein, and Robert E. Goodin (Oxford: Oxford University Press, 2008), 689–708.

4. Seyla Benhabib, "The Legitimacy of Human Rights," *Daedalus* (Summer 2008): 94–104; Tom Christiano, "Is Democratic Legitimacy Possible for International Institutions?" in *Global Democracy: Normative and Empirical Perspectives*, ed. Daniele Archibugui, Mathias Koenig-Archibugui, and Rafaelle Marchetti (Cambridge: Cambridge University Press, 2012), 69–95.

5. On the sociology of law, see, for instance, Tom Tyler, *Why People Obey the Law* (Princeton, NJ: Princeton University Press, 2006). In world politics, see Harold Hongu Koh, "Why Do Nations Obey International Law?" *Law Journal* 106 (1997): 2599–659; Ian Hurd *After Anarchy: Legitimacy and Power in the UN Security Council* (Princeton, NJ: Princeton University Press, 2007). Thomas Franck says, "A partial definition of legitimacy adapted to the international system could be formulated thus:

a property of a rule or rule-making institution which itself exerts a pull towards compliance on those addressed normatively." Thomas M. Franck, *The Power of Legitimacy among Nations* (Oxford: Oxford University Press, 1990) 16.

6. See Fuad Zarbiyev, "A Genealogy of Textualism in Treaty Interpretation," in *Interpretation in International Law*, ed. Andrea Bianchi, Daniel Peat, and Matthew Windsor (Oxford: Oxford University Press, 2015), 251–67; Jens Olesen, "Towards a Politics of Hermeneutics," in *Interpretation in International Law*, ed. Andrea Bianchi, Daniel Peat, and Matthew Windsor (Oxford: Oxford University Press, 2015), 311–30.

7. See, among others, David P. Forsythe, *The Politics of Prisoner Abuse: The United States and Enemy Prisoners after 9/11* (Cambridge: Cambridge University Press, 2011); Jane Mayer, *The Dark Side: The Inside Story of How the War on Terror Turned into a War on American Ideals* (New York: Doubleday, 2008); Philippe Sands, *Lawless World: Making and Breaking International Law* (New York Penguin, 2006); Harold Hongju Koh, "Can the President Be Torturer in Chief?" *Indiana Law Journal* 81 (2006): 1145–67. On their resonance today, see Charlie Savage, *Power Wars: Inside Obama's Post-9/11 Presidency* (Boston: Little, Brown and Company, 2015).

8. This model is advanced in Franck, *The Power of Legitimacy among Nations*; Robert O. Keohane, "Global Governance and Democratic Accountability," in *Taming Globalization: Frontiers of Governance*, ed. David Held and Mattias Koenig-Archibugi (Cambridge, UK: Polity, 2003), 130–59. See the essays in Føllesdal, Schaffer, and Ulfstein, *The Legitimacy of International Human Rights Regimes*.

9. Darius Rejali, for instance, documents how liberal states have devised new procedures of torture that leave little physical evidence that might then be used to prove a legal violation. Darius Rejali, *Torture and Democracy* (Princeton, NJ: Princeton University Press, 2007). See also Jinee Lokaneeta, *Transnational Torture: Law, Violence, and State Power in the United States and India* (New York: NYU Press, 2011).

10. "Convention against Torture and Other Cruel, Inhuman, or Degrading Treatment or Punishment," 1984, accessed March 13 2017, http://www.ohchr.org/EN/ProfessionalInterest/Pages/CAT.aspx; "Geneva Conventions and Commentaries," accessed March 13, 2017, http://www.icrc.org/eng/war-and-law/treaties-customary-law/geneva-conventions/index.jsp. Of special relevance below is the Third Convention: "Convention (III) Relative to the Treatment of Prisoners of War," 1949, accessed March 13, 2017, http://www.icrc.org/ihl.nsf/FULL/375?OpenDocument.

11. The International Criminal Tribunal for the Former Yugoslavia in Furundzjia said "that torture is prohibited by a peremptory norm of international law," and if this is right, then even states that decline to sign any of the relevant treaties are still obligated to refrain from torture as a matter of law. See Erika de Wet, "The Prohibition of Torture as an International Legal Norm of Jus Cogens and Its Implications for National and Customary Law," *European Journal of International Law* 15, no. 1 (2004): 97–121.

12. "International Convention on Civil and Political Rights," 1976, accessed March 13, 2017, http://www.ohchr.org/EN/ProfessionalInterest/Pages/CCPR.aspx; "American Convention on Human Rights," 1969, accessed March 13, 2017, http://www.oas.org/dil/treaties_B-32_American_Convention_on_Human_Rights.htm. The Ameri-

can Convention on Human Rights is open to members of the Organization of American States.

13. Charter of the United Nations Preamble; see also Article 56.

14. See Gerry Simpson, *Law, War, and Crime: Trials and the Reinvention of International Law* (Cambridge, UK: Polity, 2007).

15. "Questions relating to the Obligation to Prosecute or Extradite (Belgium v. Senegal)," accessed March 13, 2107, http://www.icj-cij.org/docket/files/144/17084 .pdf.

16. Habrè was eventually tried and convicted by an extraordinary court in Senegal created in conjunction with the African Union and began a life sentence in prison there in 2016.

17. Rome Statute of the International Criminal Court, Article 25(1).

18. See David Scheffer, "Criminal Justice," in *The Oxford Handbook of International Organizations*, ed. Jacob Katz Cogan, Ian Hurd, and Ian Johnstone (Oxford: Oxford University Press, 2016): 282-302.

19. Human Rights Watch, "Shielded from Justice: Police Brutality and Accountability in the United States," 1998, accessed February 6, 2013, http://www.hrw.org /legacy/reports98/police/uspo53.htm.

20. Andrea Liese, "Exceptional Necessity: How Liberal Democracies Contest the Prohibition of Torture and Ill-Treatment When Countering Terrorism," *Journal of International Law and International Relations* 5, no. 1 (2009): 21.

21. See, for instance, Interim Transitional National Council of Libya, press release, Benghazi, Libya, March 25, 2011.

22. On antitorture rules as evidence of moral progress in world politics, see, for instance, Richard Jolly, Louis Emmerij, and Thomas G. Weiss, eds. *UN Ideas That Changed the World* (Bloomington: Indiana University Press, 2009).

23. Louise Arbour, "On Terrorists and Torturers" (statement by the UN high commissioner for human rights, December 7, 2005), cited in Liese, "Exceptional Necessity," 17.

24. Among many others, see, for instance, Michael B. Mukasey, "The CIA Interrogations Followed the Law," *Wall Street Journal*, December 16, 2014.

25. Michael Ignatieff, *The Lesser Evil: Political Ethics in an Age of Terror* (Princeton, NJ: Princeton University Press, 2004); Forsythe, *The Politics of Prisoner Abuse*, chap. 7.

26. Alan Dershowitz, "The Torture Warrant: A Response to Professor Strauss," *New York Law School Law Review* 48, nos. 1–2 (2003–4): 275–94.

27. On the former, see Ian Hurd, *After Anarchy: Legitimacy and Power in the UN Security Council* (Princeton, NJ: Princeton University Press, 2007); Erik Voeten, "The Political Origins of the UN Security Council's Ability to Legitimize the Use of Force," *International Organization* 59, no. 3 (2005): 527–58. On the latter, see Allen Buchanan, *Justice, Legitimacy, and Self-Determination: Moral Foundations for International Law* (Oxford: Oxford University Press, 2007); Corneliu Bjola, "Legitimating the Use of Force in International Politics: A Communicative Action Perspective," *European Journal of International Relations* 11, no. 2 (2005): 266–303.

28. On the behavioral consequences of the third face of power, see, for instance, John Gaventa, *Power and Powerlessness: Quiescence and Rebellion in an Appalachian Valley* (Champaign: University of Illinois Press, 1982).

29. This is put to use to determine when preemptive force is legitimate by Michael Doyle in *Striking First: Preemption and Prevention in International Conflict* (Princeton, NJ: Princeton University Press, 2008).

30. Tyler, *Why People Obey the Law.*

31. Buchanan, *Justice, Legitimacy, and Self-Determination.*

32. Johan Karlsson Schaffer, Andreas Føllesdal, and Geir Ulfstein, "International Human Rights Regimes and the Challenge of Legitimacy," in *The Legitimacy of International Human Rights Regimes: Legal, Political, and Philosophical Perspectives*, ed. Andreas Føllesdal, Johan Karlsson Schaffer, and Geir Ulfstein (Cambridge: Cambridge University Press, 2014), 1–31.

33. See, for instance, "The Cingranelli and Richards (CIRI) Human Rights Data Set," accessed March 14, 2017, http://www.binghamton.edu/cdp/ciri.html. See also Rejali, *Torture and Democracy.*

34. On the human costs of these abstract concepts, see Mohamedou Ould Slahi, *Guantanamo Diary* (Boston: Little, Brown and Company, 2015); Center for Victims of Torture, "Torture Rehabilitation and Research Bibliography," accessed January 26, 2016, http://www.cvt.org/sites/cvt.org/files/u18/CVT%20Torture%20Rehabilitation%20and%20Research%20Biobliography.pdf. For arguments about the impact on international law and treaties, see Oona A. Hathaway, "Why Do Countries Commit to Human Rights Treaties?" *Journal of Conflict Resolution* 51, no. 4 (2007): 588–621.

35. George W. Bush, news conference, Panama City, November 7, 2005.

36. James Masters, "Donald Trump Says Torture 'Absolutely Works'—but Does It?" CNN.com, January 26, 2017.

37. Eric Holder, US attorney general, testimony to US Senate, May 4, 2011; American Society of International Law, "U.S. State Dept. Legal Advisor Lays Out Obama Administration Position on Engagement, 'Law of 9/11,'" press release, March 25, 2010.

38. Liese, "Exceptional Necessity"; Philippe Sands, *Torture Team: Rumsfeld's Memo and the Betrayal of American Values* (Basingstoke, UK: Palgrave Macmillan, 2008); Anne-Marie Slaughter, "ASIL Leaders' Views," *American Society of International Law*, accessed February 6, 2013, http://www.asil.org/slaughter-leaderview.cfm; "What Do Top Legal Experts Say about the Syria Strikes?" justsecurity.org, April 7, 2017.

39. Michael J. Kelly, "Charting America's Return to Public International Law under the Obama Administration," *Journal of National Security Law and Policy* 3, no. 2 (2009): 239–62. See also Savage, *Power Wars.*

40. This is documented in, among other places, Center for Constitutional Rights, "Report on Torture and Cruel, Inhuman, and Degrading Treatment of Prisoners at Guantánamo Bay, Cuba," accessed February 6, 2013, http://ccrjustice.org/files/Report_ReportOnTorture.pdf; Forsythe, *The Politics of Prisoner Abuse*; Sands, *Torture Team.* As I argue below, the United States sought to create ambiguity over

whether its actions qualified as torture as a matter of international law; this does not preclude acknowledging the existence of torture as a factual matter.

41. Mayer, *The Dark Side*; Forsythe, *The Politics of Prisoner Abuse.*

42. Curtis A. Bradley, "The Bush Administration and International Law: Too Much Lawyering and Too Little Diplomacy," *Duke Journal of Constitutional Law and Public Policy* 59 (2009): 57–75.

43. Charlotte Epstein has said "a primary determination in the fixing of an object's meaning is the evacuation of what it is not: in the Spinozist formula, logically 'every determination is a negation.'" Charlotte Epstein, *The Power of Words in International Relations: Birth of an Anti-Whaling Discourse* (Cambridge, MA: MIT Press, 2008), 9.

44. George W. Bush, memorandum from President George W. Bush to Vice President Dick Cheney and others, "Humane Treatment of al Qaeda and Taliban Detainees," February 7, 2002.

45. Bradley, "The Bush Administration and International Law."

46. "Memorandum from Jay S. Bybee, Assistant Attorney General, to Alberto Gonzales, Counsel to the President, re: Standards for Conduct for Interrogation," August 1, 2002, accessed February 6, 2013, http://www.justice.gov/olc/docs/memo-gonzales-aug2002.pdf.

47. BBC News, "U.S. Judge Steps in to Torture Row," February 12, 2008, accessed February 6, 2013, http://news.bbc.co.uk/2/hi/americas/7239748.stm.

48. "Memorandum from Jay S. Bybee"; John Yoo, *War by Other Means: An Insider's Account of the War on Terrorism* (New York: Grove Press, 2006). This is different than the argument about a kind of 'state of exception' in which the President is given discretion to violate the law. For instance, Jack Goldsmith defended the proposition that torture could be legal in situations "in which the President believed that exceeding the law was necessary in an emergency." Jack Goldsmith, *The Terror Presidency*, 2007, 148, cited in M. P. Scharf, "International Law and the Torture Memos," *Case Western Reserve Journal of International Law* 42 (2009): 349.

49. For a key example, see Koh, "Can the President Be Torturer in Chief?"

50. See, for instance, John F. Murphy, *The United States and the Rule of Law in International Affairs* (Cambridge: Cambridge University Press, 2004). Tom Bingham says, "The Constitution of the United States was a crucial staging-post in the history of the rule of law." Tom Bingham, *The Rule of Law* (New York: Penguin, 2011).

51. "Nobel Lecture by Barack H. Obama," Oslo, December 10, 2009, accessed February 6, 2013, http://www.nobelprize.org/nobel_prizes/peace/laureates/2009/obama-lecture_en.html.

52. G. John Ikenberry, *Liberal Leviathan: The Origins, Crisis, and Transformation of the American World Order* (Princeton, NJ: Princeton University Press, 2011).

53. See, for instance, David Cole, *Engines of Liberty: The Power of Citizen Activists to Make Constitutional Law* (New York: Basic Books, 2016).

54. At Guantanamo Bay at least, many accounts suggest less mistreatment over time. Forsythe, *The Politics of Prisoner Abuse*; Slahi, *Guantanamo Diary.*

55. Neil MacCormick, "Argument and Interpretation in Law," *Argumentation* 6,

no. 1 (1993): 19, cited in Scott Veitch, *Law and Irresponsibility: On the Legitimation of Human Suffering* (Abingdon, UK: Routledge-Cavendish, 2007), 77.

56. Kenneth Abbott and Duncan Snidal, "Hard and Soft Law in International Governance," *International Organization* 54, no. 3 (2000): 429.

57. Ingo Venzke, "Legal Contestation about 'Enemy Combatants'—On the Exercise of Power in Legal Interpretation," *Journal of International Law and International Relations* 5, no. 1 (2009): 160 (emphasis removed).

58. On the rise of a professional class attached to international law, see Anne-Marie Slaughter, *A New World Order* (Princeton, NJ: Princeton University Press, 2004); David Kennedy, *A World of Struggle: How Power, Law, and Expertise Shape Global Political Economy* (Princeton, NJ: Princeton University Press, 2016); Martti Koskenniemi, *The Gentle Civilizer of Nations: The Rise and Fall of International Law, 1870–1960* (Cambridge: Cambridge University Press, 2001); Frédéric Mégret, "Thinking about What International Lawyers 'Do': An Examination of the Laws of War as a Field of Professional Practice," in *The Law of International Lawyers: Reading Martti Koskenniemi*, ed. Wouter Werner, Marieke de Hoon, and Alexis Galán Ávila (Cambridge: Cambridge University Press, 2015).

59. Veitch, *Law and Irresponsibility*, 3.

60. On the link between juridification and human welfare, see Teitel, *Humanity's Law*. I explore a case of this "reversal" in Mara Pillinger, Ian Hurd, and Michael N. Barnett, "How to Get Away with Cholera: The UN, Haiti, and International Law," *Perspectives on Politics*, March 2016, accessed March 15, 2017, http://www.political sciencenow.com/how-to-get-away-with-cholera-the-un-haiti-and-international -law/.

61. See Bonnie Honig, *Political Theory and the Displacement of Politics* (Ithaca, NY: Cornell University Press, 1993).

62. Brian Z. Tamanaha, *On the Rule of Law: History, Politics, Theory* (Cambridge: Cambridge University Press, 2004).

63. Madeleine Albright, "Building a Bipartisan Foreign Policy" (address at Rice Memorial Center, Rice University, Houston, Texas, February 7, 1997), accessed February 11, 2013, http://www.womenspeecharchive.org/files/Building_a_Bipartisan _Foreign_Polic_D3FED68BA927D.pdf.

64. On the power of "indeterminacy," see Franck, *The Power of Legitimacy among Nations*. On enhancing the legitimacy of rule following, see Andreas Føllesdal, "The Legitimacy Deficits of the Human Rights Judiciary: Elements and Implications of a Normative Theory," *Theoretical Inquiries in Law* 14, no. 2 (2013): 339–60. On norm-following states, see Judith Kelley, "Who Keeps International Commitments and Why? The International Criminal Court and Bilateral Non-Surrender Agreements," *American Political Science Association* 3, no. 101 (2007): 573–89.

65. For an in-depth exploration of this idea, see Benjamin Schonthal, *Buddhism, Politics and the Limits of Law* (New York: Cambridge University Press, 2016).

66. Emilie Hafner-Burton, David G. Victor, and Yonatan Lupu, "Political Science Research on International Law: The State of the Field," *American Journal of International Law* 106, no. 1 (2012): 47–97.

67. Hedley Bull, *The Anarchical Society: A Study of Order in International Politics* (New York: Columbia University Press 1977), 150.

68. Harold Hongju Koh, statement to American Society of International Law, March 25, 2010, accessed April 14, 2017, http://www.cfr.org/international-law/legal-adviser-kohs-speech-obama-administration-international-law-march-2010/p22300.

69. Peter Lindseth, *Power and Legitimacy: Reconciling Europe and the Nation-State* (Oxford: Oxford University Press, 2010), 21–22.

70. Venzke, "Legal Contestation about 'Enemy Combatants.'" "Successful interpretations, that is, interpretations that find acceptance, can be thus be conceived as expressions of power" (162).

Chapter 7: The Empire of International Legalism

1. Judith Shklar, *Legalism: Law, Morals, and Political Trials* (Cambridge, MA: Harvard University Press, 1986). Eric Posner uses the term differently, with "global legalism" to refer to the attempt to create what he sees as "law without government" at the global level. For Shklar, Hannah Arendt, and the other scholars I rely on here, legalism is a form of governance and not something separate from it. Eric Posner, *The Perils of Global Legalism* (Chicago: University of Chicago Press, 2009).

2. G. John Ikenberry, *Liberal Leviathan: The Origins, Crisis, and Transformation of the American World Order* (Princeton, NJ: Princeton University Press, 2011), 345.

3. Samantha Besson, "Whose Constitution(s)? International Law, Constitutionalism, and Democracy," in *Ruling the World? Constitutionalism, International Law, and Global Governance*, ed. Jeffrey L. Dunoff and Joel P. Trachtman (New York: Cambridge University Press, 2009), 389. For broader debates about the concept, see Andreas L. Paulus, "The International Legal System as a Constitution," in *Ruling the World? Constitutionalism, International Law, and Global Governance*, ed. Jeffrey L. Dunoff and Joel P. Trachtman (New York: Cambridge University Press, 2009), 69–112; Besson, "Whose Constitution(s)?"; discussion in chapter 2. See also discussions starting in 2012 in the journal *Global Constitutionalism*.

4. Antje Wiener, *A Theory of Contestation* (Heidelberg: Springer, 2014), 1.

5. Kenneth N. Waltz, *Theory of International Politics* (Hoboken, NJ: Wiley, 1979), 88.

6. James Crawford and Martti Koskenniemi, introduction to *The Cambridge Companion to International Law*, ed. James Crawford and Martti Koskenniemi (Cambridge: Cambridge University Press, 2012), 8–9.

7. Timothy Sinclair, *Global Governance* (Cambridge, UK: Polity, 2012), 9.

8. See James Owen Weatherall, *Void: The Strange Physics of Nothing* (New Haven, CT: Yale University Press, 2016).

9. Siba N. Grovogui, "This State of Independence Shall Be: Africa, the West, and the Responsibility to Protect," *Relaciones Internacionales* 26 (2014): 137-155.

10. Gareth Evans and Mohamed Sahnoun, "The Responsibility to Protect," *Foreign Affairs* 81, no. 6 (2002): 101.

11. Michael N. Barnett, "Introduction: International Paternalism: Framing the

Debate," in *Paternalism beyond Borders*, ed. Michael N. Barnett (Cambridge: Cambridge University Press, 2017), 4.

12. Self-determination of peoples is widely cited as having the status of *jus cogens* in contemporary international law. Anthony Anghie, *Imperialism, Sovereignty, and the Making of International Law* (Cambridge: Cambridge University Press, 2005). On the US context, see Benjamin Allen Coates, *Legalist Empire: International Law and American Foreign Relations in the Early Twentieth Century* (Ithaca, NY: Cornell University Press, 2016). On historical developments in these issues, see James Gathii, "Imperialism, Colonialism, and International Law," *Buffalo Law Review* 54 (2006–7): 1013–66.

13. Jennifer Welsh, "Civilian Protection in Libya: Putting Coercion and Controversy Back into RtoP," *Ethics and International Affairs* 25, no. 3 (2011): 255–62; Ian Hurd, "Is Humanitarian Intervention Legal? The Rule of Law in an Incoherent World," *Ethics and International Affairs* 25, no. 3 (2011): 293–313. These ideas are central to Martha Finnemore, *The Purpose of Intervention: Changing Beliefs about the Use of Force* (Ithaca, NY: Cornell University Press, 2003). Finnemore, though, does not use the language of paternalism.

14. Stephen Hopgood, "Modernity at the Cutting Edge: Human Rights Meets FGM," in *Paternalism beyond Borders*, ed. Michael N. Barnett (Cambridge: Cambridge University Press, 2017). For a critical discussion, see John M. Hobson, "Eurocentric Pitfalls and Paradoxes of International Paternalism: Decolonizing Liberal Humanitarianism 2.0," in *Paternalism beyond Borders*, ed. Michael N. Barnett (Cambridge: Cambridge University Press, 2017).

15. Robert Paul Wolff, "The Conflict between Authority and Autonomy," in *Authority*, ed. Joseph Raz (New York: NYU Press, 1990), 20.

16. B. S. Chimni, "International Institutions Today: An Emerging World State in the Making," *European Journal of International Law* 51, no. 1 (2004): 1–37. See also William Walters, *Governmentality: Critical Encounters* (Abingdon, UK: Routledge, 2012).

17. Alexander E. Wendt, "Why a World-State Is Inevitable," *European Journal of International Relations* 9, no. 4 (2003): 505. Wendt sets additional conditions on a world state, including the existence of a universal security community and the absence of interstate -threat, which I don't address here yet that lead him to conclude that a world state is "clearly some way off" (505). I suggest elsewhere that these may already be realized in the UN Security Council. Ian Hurd, *After Anarchy: Legitimacy and Power in the UN Security Council* (Princeton, NJ: Princeton University Press, 2007); Ian Hurd, "UN Security Council," in *The Oxford Handbook of International Security*, ed. Alexandra Gheciu and William Wohlforth (Oxford: Oxford University Press, 2017).

18. Ikenberry, *Liberal Leviathan*, 67.

19. On the controversies around this, see A. Mark Weisburd, "The International Court of Justice and the Concept of State Practice," *University of Pennsylvania Journal of International Law* 31, no. 2 (2009): 295–372.

20. Hurd, "Is Humanitarian Intervention Legal?"

21. See Andrea Bianchi, Daniel Peat, and Matthew Windsor, eds., *Interpretation in International Law* (Oxford: Oxford University Press, 2015).

22. Ikenberry, *Liberal Leviathan*, chap. 2.

23. Samuel Moyn, "Soft Sells: On Liberal Internationalism," *Nation*, September 14, 2011, accessed March 15, 2017, https://www.thenation.com/article/soft-sells-liberal-internationalism/.

24. This is charted in Gerry Simpson, *Great Powers and Outlaw States: Unequal Sovereigns in the International Legal Order* (Cambridge: Cambridge University Press, 2004). B. S. Murty notes that "the influence which great Powers exercise in the development of customary law is definitely more marked than the influence of small Powers." B. S. Murty, *The International Law of Diplomacy: The Diplomatic Instrument and World Politics* (Leiden: Martinus Nijhoff, 1989), 585. Koremenos says that "powerful states want their asymmetric power reflected in the terms of the agreement, but this desire is not synonymous with having complete control." Barbara Koremenos, *The Continent of International Law: Explaining Agreement Design* (Cambridge: Cambridge University Press, 2016), 295. See also Hurd, "The UN Security Council."

25. On the first, see Hersch Lauterpacht, *The Function of Law in the International Community* (1933), cited in Thomas M. Franck, *Recourse to Force: State Action against Threats and Armed Attacks* (Cambridge: Cambridge University Press, 2002); Oona A. Hathaway and Scott Shapiro, *The Worst Crime of All* (New York: Simon and Schuster, 2017). On the second, see Bull, *The Anarchical Society*.

26. Ian Hurd, "Enchanted and Disenchanted International Law," *Global Policy* 2, no. 1 (2016): 1–7.

27. Shklar, *Legalism*, 2.

28. Bonnie Honig, *Political Theory and the Displacement of Politics* (Ithaca, NY: Cornell University Press, 1993), 27.

29. Hannah Arendt, *Eichmann in Jerusalem: A Report on the Banality of Evil* (New York: Viking, 1963).

30. Ingo Venzke, "Is Interpretation in International Law a Game?" in *Interpretation in International Law*, ed. Andrea Bianchi, Daniel Peat, and Matthew Windsor (Oxford: Oxford University Press, 2015), 355.

31. Oona Hathaway, "Why We Need International Law," *Nation*, November 1, 2007.

32. Thomas L. Friedman, *The Lexus and the Olive Tree: Understanding Globalization* (New York: Picador, 1999), cited in Ronnie D. Lipschutz, "Imitations of Empire," *Global Environmental Politics* 4, no. 2 (2004): 21; Stephen G. Brooks and William C. Wohlforth, *America Abroad: The United States' Global Role in the 21st Century* (Oxford: Oxford University Press, 2016), 160.

33. Friedrich List, *National System of Political Economy* (Philadelphia: J. B. Lippincott, 1856), chap. 4. He said, among other things, "Theorists have since pretended that England has become rich and powerful, not on account, but in spite of her commercial policy [that is, infant industry protection]. It might as well be maintained that a tree becomes stronger and more productive, not on account, but in spite of the attention and helps which it received in its early growth" (114).

34. "Vladimir Putin's Outlaw State," *New York Times*, September 29, 2016, A26. On the possible draft executive order on the United Nations and multilateralism, see Anne Gearan and Juliet Ellperin, "Trump Administration Could Cut Funding to United Nations," *Washington Post*, January 25, 2017.

35. This sets aside a large discussion over the many uses and connotations of this term. My use follows in particular Hardt and Negri, *Empire*; Chimni, "International Institutions Today"; Lipschutz, "Imitations of Empire." It links up with Schmitt on nomos. For other ways of conceiving of the term, see Paul A. Kramer, "Power and Connection: Imperial Histories of the United States and the World," *American Historical Review* 116, no. 5 (2011): 1348–91.

36. Carl Schmitt, *The Nomos of the Earth in the International Law of the Jus Publicum Europaeum* (Candor, NY: Telos Press, 2003), 78. Robert Cover used nomos to describe the normative universe of concepts, stories, rules, and taken for granteds in which people operate. Robert M. Cover, "Nomos and Narrative," *Harvard Law Review* 97, no. 4 (1983–84): 4–68.

INDEX

Abbott, Kenneth, 124
Abraham, Ronny, 147n51
acquiescence and social power, theory of, 114
Adler, Emmanuel, 53
Afghanistan, 72, 73, 92, 120, 159n41
aggression, 35, 49, 51, 75, 78, 81, 131. *See also* war
Albright, Madeleine, 126
Alter, Karen, 24, 139n2
Alvarez, José E., 41
American Convention on Human Rights (1969), 108
Amnesty International, 94
anarchy, 4, 36–37, 131–32
Arbour, Louise, 113
Arendt, Hannah, 135, 173n1
Argentina, 67
assassinations, 14, 165n39
atrocities, prevention of, 52
Australia, 33, 52
Aznar-Gomez, Mariano J., 86

balance of power, 132
Bauman, Zygmunt, 52
Belgium, 110–11, 159–60n50
Belgium v. Senegal, 35, 110–11
Berlin, disco bombing in, 161n65
Besson, Samantha, 49, 130
Betts, Alexander, 167n2
bill of rights, 23
Bingham, Tom, 27–28
Bolton, John, 88
Bosnia, 72
Bourdieu, Pierre, 53
Brooks, Rosa, 12, 157n19

Brooks, Stephen, 136
Brunkhorst, Hauke, 142–43n37; *Critical Theory of Legal Revolutions,* 82
Brunnée, Jutta, 53, 55
Buchanan, Allen, 115
Bull, Hedley, 36, 37, 63, 126
Bush, George W., 117–18
Bush administration, 18, 105, 106, 118–19, 121, 134
Bybee memo, 121
Byers, Michael, 58, 63, 70, 81, 158n37

Caroline case (1837), 69
CAT. *See* Convention against Torture and Other Cruel, Inhuman, or Degrading Treatment (CAT)
Center for Justice and Accountability, 152n5
chemical weapons, 49
Chesterman, Simon, 22
Chimni, B. S., 65, 134
China, 49
citizens: defense of abroad, 74; government *vs.*, 20; law as binding on, 12, 24; limited government authority over, 36; obligation of to follow law, 25–26; and Rome Statute of International Criminal Court, 111; and rule of law, 21, 22
civilians, 13–14, 73, 86, 90–91, 93
Coalition for the International Criminal Court, 152n5
Coates, Benjamin, 55
codification, 6–7, 30, 31–33
coercion, 1, 114
Cold War, 72

A NOTE ON THE TYPE

This book has been composed in Adobe Text and Gotham. Adobe Text, designed by Robert Slimbach for Adobe, bridges the gap between fifteenth- and sixteenth-century calligraphic and eighteenth-century Modern styles. Gotham, inspired by New York street signs, was designed by Tobias Frere-Jones for Hoefler & Co.